MW00465964

Cold Lead

Only known photograph of Tom Blanck, taken by Seattle photographer Frank LaRoche on October 5, 1894. *Author's collection.*

Cold Lead

The Life, Times and Death of 1890s Killer Tom Blanck

by Mark Dugan

hancock

house

ISBN 0-88839-559-0
EAN 9780888395597
Copyright © 2006 Mark Dugan

Cataloging in Publication Data

Dugan, Mark, 1939–
    Cold lead : the life, times and death of 1890s killer Tom Blanck
/ Mark Dugan.
Includes bibliographical references and index.

ISBN 0-88839-559-0

    1. Blanck, Tom. 2. Outlaws—West (U.S.)—Biography.
3. Murderers—West (U.S.)—Biography. I. Title.

HV6248.B545D84 2006   364.15'52'092   C2005-906574-5

Editor: Nancy Miller
Production: Stefanie Eastcott
Cover design: Stefanie Eastcott

Published simultaneously in Canada and the United States by

HANCOCK HOUSE PUBLISHERS LTD.
19313 Zero Avenue, Surrey, B.C. Canada V3S 9R9
(604) 538-1114 Fax (604) 538-2262

HANCOCK HOUSE PUBLISHERS
1431 Harrison Avenue, Blaine, WA U.S.A. 98230-5005
(604) 538-1114 Fax (604) 538-2262

Website: **www.hancockhouse.com**
Email: **sales@hancockhouse.com**

Contents

Dedication

To Nancy Schaffer, Schenectady Public Library, Schenectady, New York, whose untiring efforts helped me solve the riddle of the identity of Tom Blanck; and thanks to all the other archivists, researchers and librarians who contributed so much to make this book a reality.

Foreword

We have all known men like the deadly subject of this work. Men of his potential for evil and destruction come in all shapes and sizes, from all sorts of backgrounds. Tom Blanck is the kid in grammar school constantly being reprimanded by the teacher for interrupting the class and stealing from his classmates. He's the thug in high school who is into petty crime and drugs and finally drops out looking for larger prey—the one you read about later in the newspapers. Or sometimes he is the sullen, quiet one just waiting to explode.

In the military he is likely to be the guy always on a drunk or selling his gear and claiming it was stolen or lost. Most of the time those in authority are too busy trying to keep up with him to look into the surroundings that produced him, even if it was their business.

He is that mean-looking character at the end of the bar, the one with the expression so easy to read. He sits there alone, in the shadows, and has "caution" written all over him. You have seen him in other bars and other places around the world. Somehow you know that he doesn't care. He will act first and think later and not give a hang how his actions affect others.

Most people have known Tom Blanck types during their life and been able to avoid them. They are all around us, but luckily most remain dormant and are never pushed, pulled or triggered into that final, dead-end black corridor leading to destruction.

It is easy to isolate Tom Blanck and a few others and dismiss them as merely legendary desperadoes of the Old West. But that is not accurate. We had Tom Blancks in prehistoric times and we have them today. We've always had them and always will. The truth is, for all the social explanations, there are bad men out there. They come from the best families and from the worst. They are rich and poor, but mostly they are mean. Carl Panzram, who spent most of his life in modern-day prisons, once put on paper the psyche he

7

shared with Tom Blanck: "I have no desire whatever to reform myself. My only desire is to reform people who try to reform me. And I believe the only way to reform people is to kill 'em."[1]

Perhaps this is another frightening characteristic of such people; they are unreasonable. They are unwilling to discuss a situation and are not logical. Often they will smile and agree with you, but you know by that smile you are wasting your breath. Things will be done their way or no way. Their viewpoint is all that matters.

Look into the face of Tom Blanck. Most mug shots of criminals show sullen men who are bitter and angry. Never mind that they have broken the law, they resent being captured and photographed. Some show fear, some shame and some defiance. Fewer still glare insolently into the camera, as if to say, "Photograph me if you will, but you will rue this day, and soon." Tom Blanck's face almost talks to you! With a bandage on his head where he has been beaten into submission, he still stares into the lens with just a whisper of a smile on his lips. Defiant, unconquered, he hasn't been caught—it is just a matter of time before he catches you! There is no humbling in that look. He wants you to know that you have him now, but not for long. Those cold eyes of Tom Blanck's are saying, "Look out for me. Watch the forest and city alleys. I'll come back. I'll return and get you if it's the last thing I do."

The celebrity status of such criminals before and after their death is a curious fact of human nature and a constant phenomenon. When rapist and kidnapper Caryl Chessman was executed at San Quentin on May 2, 1960, he had been the recipient of a tremendous ballyhoo raised by the press and a coterie of the public who were opposed to the death penalty. His book, *Cell 2455, Death Row*, had received much attention also. The hand wringing of various sob sisters did nothing to change the opinion of the men who had to deal with this monster, however. Warden Clinton Duffy, a humane man, remarked: "I knew (him) well, and if he is ever recognized as a martyr it will be a travesty. Chessman was one of the most dangerous men I ever knew, for he had combined the brains of a savant with the morals of a degenerate.... He charmed almost every outsider he met during his twelve years on death row, but he hated them all.... In death row he was a tough prisoner to handle—mean, demanding, contemptuous, arrogant, and defiant.... Chessman could build a very plausible case on an utterly fictitious premise... He found it com-

8

paratively easy to sell himself to those who never saw him at his worst."[2]

Mark Dugan has told Blanck's story well. Without saying so he has warned us all to look around and be on guard against the Tom Blancks of the world. And he reminds us also that in this or any age, we can only have admiration and respect for the lawmen entrusted with the capture and containment of the desperadoes exemplified by the protagonist of this exciting saga of the closing days of the Old West.

—WILLIAM B. SECREST
Fresno, California

[1] Panzram, Carl, *Killer: A Journal of Murder*, edited by Thomas E. Gaddis and James O. Long, New York: Macmillan, 1970.

[2] Nichols, Nancy Ann, *San Quentin Inside the Walls*, San Quentin: San Quentin Museum Press, 1991.

Preface

I owe a debt of gratitude to California historian and author John Boessenecker for this story. In 1988, John made a suggestion that I check into the career of Tom Blanck, stating that it looked like a good story. John had read the condensed version of Blanck's escapades in Thomas Duke's book, *Celebrated Criminal Cases Of America*, and had another California historian and author, Bill Secrest, who also saw merit in the story, send me a photocopy of Duke's account. I agreed with John and Bill, and immediately started researching Tom Blanck. I got more than I bargained for.

As my research of this virtually unknown story progressed, I realized that Tom Blanck was not the stereotypical gunman of the Old West. He was an extremely dangerous antisocial psychopathic killer, and yet he actually gained the idolization that the myriads of western films and television productions have bestowed on their fictionalized desperados.

This characterization of the nineteenth-century western "gunfighter" has been flashed before the public too many times to count. He is a tall, reserved man with little to say, but when he does talk his audience better listen to him. He can shoot the center out of a dime at thirty paces. He is a tarnished hero—not all good but not all bad either. In the end he usually gets the most beautiful woman in town and hangs up his guns. Then there comes a time when the good citizens of the town need his services, and for a short time he is hell-on-wheels again.

Tom Blanck had none of the above qualities. He fits no one's image of a gunman of the Old West, Hollywood type or otherwise. There is no glory, no shoot-outs at the OK Corral, no *High Noons* and no John Waynes, nevertheless Blanck's story proves just as dramatic as any Hollywood scenario. Tom Blanck is no different than the remorseless killer that walks our streets today. He just happened to live and die during the last decade of the nineteenth century. Had he lived in current times, this savage street brawler and cold-blooded murderer would have had writers of contemporary crime thrillers cutting each other's throats just to get his story.

The stage is now set for the life, the times and the death of Tom Blanck, who really could shoot the center out of a dime at thirty feet. The reader will likely not like him; however, this is reality—it is the story of a true killer of the Old West. And yet, he is no more than a mirror image of the murderers that plague today's world. And that is the point of all this; customs change, habits change, life styles change, but people do not change. Tom Blanck was neither unique in the nineteenth century nor was he an exception to the rule, except for his unerring shooting ability. Men like Tom Blanck have existed since the beginning of time.

Acknowledgments

Appreciation encompasses more people than just those who contribute to the research of a book. Encouragement and support are just as important, and for these reasons I would like to extend my gratitude to the following North Carolinians: Jan Palmer, Boone; Jimmie Owens, Boone; Charles and Betty Church, Valle Crucis; Suzanne Moineau, Boone; Marvin Williamsen and Richard Hudson, Appalachian State University, Boone; Siggie Fox, Fairview; Eliza Bishop, Caldwell Community College, Lenoir; and, in memory of Rachael Rivers Coffey, Boone.

Without research assistance from the following people, this book could not have been completed:

CANADA: Susan Hart, British Columbia Archives and Records Service, Victoria; Roberta Griffiths, David Thompson Library, Nelson; James M. Whalen, National Archives of Canada, Ottawa.

CALIFORNIA: John Boessenecker, San Francisco; Bill Secrest, Fresno.

IDAHO: Ginger Schneider, Weiser Public Library, Weiser.

MONTANA: Dave Walter, Montana Historical Society Library, Helena.

NEW YORK: Reverend Robert LeFevre and Beverly Sanges of Saint John the Baptist Catholic Church, Schenectady; Diana Lee Fontaine, Schenectady County Clerk's Office; Larry Hart, Schenectady City/County Historian; Elsie M. Maddaus, Archivist/Librarian, Schenectady County Historical Society.

NORTH CAROLINA: Betty Burkett, Diana Moody, Bob Nussle, Mike Rominger, Dr. William A. Derick, Jr. and Dr. Carl R. Nordstrom, Appalachian State University, Boone; Sana Gaffney, Boone; Dr. Geraldine Powell, Asheville; Evelyn Johnson, Watauga County Library, Boone.

WASHINGTON STATE: Dave Hastings, Division of Archives and Records Management, Olympia; Gary P. Fitterer, Kirkland; Jean

Engerman, Washington State Library, Olympia; Ernie Dornfeld, King County Archives, Seattle; Nancy G. Compau, Spokane Public Library, Spokane; Carolyn Farnum, Seattle; Bert Butterworth, Seattle; Dave Daly, Seattle.

Special thanks to Andrea MacDonald, Port Orchard, Washington, who furnished me with the needed info on the burial site of Tom Blanck in the King County Hospital (Duwamish) Cemetery. I also extend gratitude to Richard Engemen of the University of Washington Libraries who went the extra mile not only furnishing much needed information, but also meticulously searching the library files until he found the only known photograph of Tom Blanck.

The cover design of a nineteenth-century postmortem scene was a combined effort of several special people. The authentic medical instruments from the last century were graciously loaned to me by president and founder Dr. Josephine E. Newell and staff member Jackie Morgan of the Old Country Doctor Museum in Bailey, North Carolina. These instruments are exact duplicates of those Coroner Askam used during the autopsy of Tom Blanck. The .45-calibre Long Colt black powder slugs are also authentic and were produced a century ago. Sergeant Humphrey Hayes of the North Carolina Department of Corrections, Watauga Correctional Center, dug them out of his collection of ammunition and, with a Smith and Wesson Model 25-5 .45 Long Colt revolver, fired several of these bullets into a barrel of water containing soaked catalogs to simulate slugs fired into a body. These represent the four bullets that killed Tom Blanck in 1895. The old-time enamel bowl was furnished by my good friend, Randy Fiemster. The antique medical table belongs to photographer Mike Rominger, who planned, staged and photographed the postmortem scene with meticulous realism.

Saving the best for last, this book would never have been finished, let alone started, without the support and help from my wife Sarah.

Compiling Tom Blanck's story, with added help from clinical psychologist David Hawley, who has drawn a psychological profile of the killer, has been a sincere enjoyment. I have written other books, but none with so much intrigue. For the readers of this book and those who contributed to the research, I hope I've done it justice, for it truly is a good story.

Introduction

It was 7:25 on a mid-March evening in 1895, five minutes before the night jailer was scheduled to come and lock down the prisoners in the desperate criminal section of the King County Jail in Seattle. A blond-headed young man with apparent strength and determination walked calmly down the open corridor that separated the two blocks of cells. Stopping at the bars surrounding the entire cellblock, he stood before the small opening used by the jailer to pass items to the prisoners.

Reaching above his head, the man untied and pulled down a small rope the prisoners used to hang their clothes on. Then he stood stark still, waiting for the jailer to appear. Outwardly he was calm, giving the impression of indifference that had been his trademark since his incarceration the previous fall. For five months he had been waiting and planning for this moment, yet the only sign of tension he exhibited was the slight, indiscernible clenching of his fingers. Inwardly he was a time bomb, and the excitement and anticipation was expressed solely in the hard glint of his cold, gray eyes.

Seconds seemed like minutes and minutes like hours to the man, as he stood motionless next to the jail bars. Finally his ears picked up the sound of the jailer's key opening the outside door to the cellblock passageway. He intently watched the approaching jailer, who was clutching a small bottle of medicine for one of the prisoners. As the jailer reached the small opening, with lightning speed the cold-eyed man covered the startled officer with a long, black, ugly-looking revolver. "Throw up your hands!" the man said in a low growl, and the luckless jailer complied.

As the jailer stood with his hands held high, the man turned to the other prisoners, who were unaware of what was transpiring, and shouted, "Stand back all of you. If anyone moves I will kill him on sight." All the prisoners knew very well how dangerous this convicted and condemned killer could be, and they unhesitatingly obeyed him. He then ordered the jailer to come close to the bars and turn his back. Giving the piece of rope to his victim, he ordered him to slip it around his left arm. Reaching through the bars, the man then tied the rope around the jailer's arm.

With his prisoner securely held, the man took the jailer's .38-calibre revolver and had him unlock both doors to the jail cell. After locking the hapless jailer in a cell, the man unlocked the door to the jailer's office. He then tossed aside his revolver, which was a fake. Turning to the other prisoners he jubilantly cried out, "All of you who want to come, follow me," and then quickly slipped out the back entrance of the jail. Eight other hardened criminals followed him.

One of the Old West's most deadly and cold-blooded killers was now loose, posing a threat not only to Seattle but to the surrounding area as well. The next day the *Seattle Post-Intelligencer* announced it to its readers with this terse headline, "TOM BLANCK FREE."[1]

---

[1] *Seattle Post-Intelligencer*, March 18, 1895.

PART 1

ROAD KILLS

CHAPTER ONE

Genesis of a Killer

Ask most readers of Western American history whom they consider the most dangerous killer of the Pacific Northwest and they will invariably reply Harry Tracy. Obviously, Tom Blanck got lost somewhere in the shuffle.

In comparison, both desperados used aliases and were petty thieves and stickup artists: Tracy holding up stores and individuals while Blanck specialized in burglary and robbing saloons. Although both men were vicious killers, this is where they differed. Tracy killed to escape or avoid capture, Blanck would kill anyone anytime, under any circumstances, whether they were lawmen or defenseless civilians.

Tracy had some redeeming traits—he was courteous and pleasant with many of his victims and was gallant with women. Blanck just shot whoever got in his way, and in the only recorded confrontation he had with a women, he threatened to throw her over a banister. Although both men are credited with killing seven men, all of Tracy's murders are verified whereas one killing Blanck confessed to is unconfirmed.

If Tracy and Blanck had not been killed, both would have continued their murderous sprees until they were stopped. However, where Tracy seemed to be able to repress his emotions, Blanck had a volatile, uncontrollable temper and, unlike his fellow desperado, was a savage brawler. Of the two men, Tom Blanck, who was clearly psychopathic, was the most dangerous.[1]

Tom Blanck gained his infamy in October, 1894, eight years before Harry Tracy came on the scene. Blanck was convicted in a King County courtroom in Seattle for murder and was sentenced to hang. During the next five months he told a fellow prisoner, and

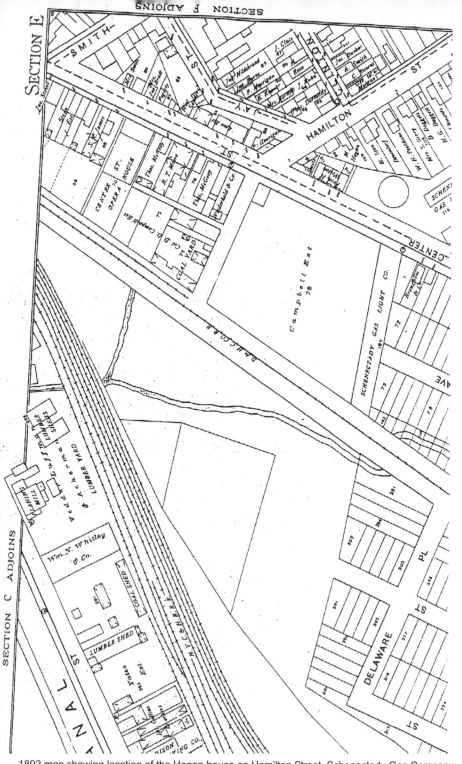

1892 map showing location of the Hogan house on Hamilton Street, Schenectady Gas Company, and railroad yards. *1892 Atlas of Schenectady, New York, R912.747 A88, Schenectady Public Library.*

inadvertently his jailer, much of his story. It was an unbelievable confession of murder and robbery across the Pacific Northwest. What is more incredulous is that most of his stories can be verified as fact, which lends credence to the rest.

His confidant and fellow prisoner in Seattle, George Howe, gave an interesting evaluation of Tom Blanck's character to the *Seattle Post-Intelligencer* in March, 1895: "There is no question, of course, that Blanck was a bad man, but on the other hand he was one of the pleasantest fellows I ever met, and generous to a fault. He was a remarkable fellow in many respects. For instance he never took a drink of liquor in his life, and was a total stranger to tobacco in any form. He didn't care much for women, either. I asked him one day what he did with his money, and he replied he used it to buy anything that caught his eye, and when he got tired of it he would throw it away. At other times he would get a crowd of boys around him and buy them candy and such stuff, and give them give them a dollar or so apiece.[2]

In addition to the assumed name Thomas Hamilton Blanck, the man killer used several other nicknames and aliases: Crazy Mike, Slim Jim, Thomas Moore, James Moore, James H. Brown, Frank Hamilton and, at the end, James Mendell, but no official in the Northwest knew his true identity. Following Blanck's death in 1895, the *Evening Star* in his hometown of Schenectady, New York, revealed that his given name was Michael Hogan.

Hogan's father was Michael Hogan, Sr., born in January, 1832, and his mother, Margaret Fox, in August, 1834. Both were Irish-born Catholics. Following thousands of their compatriots who immigrated to the United States to escape the Irish potato famine, Michael Hogan and Margaret Fox arrived in New York on October 9, 1852. They were married in 1855, undoubtedly in Saint John the Baptist Church, Schenectady's first established Catholic Church. On April 8, 1856, Michael, Sr. was naturalized in the Supreme Court of Schenectady.

In 1857, the Hogans lived on North Front Street and Michael, Sr. worked as a laborer. In 1862 he was employed as a gasman and the family moved to Franklin Street. The Hogans moved for the final time in 1864 to 2 Hamilton Street in the 5th Ward. Michael, Sr. worked as a fireman until 1867 when he opened a blacksmith shop, an occupation he followed the remainder of his life.

Photograph taken in winter of 1880 of Hamilton Street, facing west towards the intersection of Centre Street. The Hogan house is the second structure on the left from Centre Street intersection. Notice the three children about the age of Michael Hogan, Jr. (Tom Blanck) in 1880 playing in front of the Hogan house. *Courtesy Larry Hart, City and County Historian, Schenectady, New York.*

From 1887 to 1890 their home address changed to 24 Hamilton Street, and from 1890 the address was listed as 416 Hamilton Street. Their house was located in Schenectady's industrial district, on the south side of Hamilton Street and two houses east of where Hamilton converged with Centre Street (now Broadway). Directly behind the Hogan home was the Schenectady Gas Company, and a block west ran the tracks of the Delaware and Hudson Railroad, and then the tracks of much larger New York Central and Hudson River Railroad. Continuing another long block west was the Erie Canal.

Young Michael appears to be the only bad seed in the typically large Irish Catholic Hogan family. Siblings Patrick, a railroad fireman, and Mary, a dressmaker, were apparently twins born in August, 1856. The other children were Kate, born 1858, a milliner; Ella, born 1860, a milliner; Charles, born 1861, a machinist; Anne, born March, 1866, a dressmaker; John, born February, 1868, a cigar maker; James, born February, 1872, a boilermaker; and Thomas J., born January, 1878, a bookkeeper.

Michael, Jr., the eighth of ten children, first saw the light of day on October 28, 1870, and was baptized by Reverend M. E. Clarke in Saint John the Baptist Catholic Church on November 6. His godparents were Thomas Trainer and Ellen McCauley. When jailed in Seattle in early October, 1894, he fudged a little when stating he was twenty-four-years-old; however, this corresponds with the 1880 Schenectady census, enumerated on June 1.[3]

There is not much known of his early life. He stated he received only a common school education (elementary school, generally consisting of six grades), and he could read and write, but he proved to be a highly intelligent man with a quick wit. He undoubtedly attended the Clinton Street Elementary School located on the corner of Clinton and Smith Streets, one block north of his home.

Another clue to his beginnings comes from the coroner's report following Michael Hogan's death in 1895. His lungs were completely covered with black spots, indicating he suffered from pneu-

Another photograph taken in winter of 1880 of Hamilton Street, facing west towards the intersection of Centre Street. The Hogan house is the second structure on the left from Centre Street intersection. *Courtesy Larry Hart, City and County Historian, Schenectady, New York.*

1920 photograph of the original structure of St. John the Baptist Catholic Church in Schenectady, New York, where Michael Hogan aka Tom Blanck was baptized in 1870. *Courtesy St. John the Baptist Catholic Church.*

moconiosis, the coal miner's disease commonly called "black lung." The coroner assumed Hogan, alias Blanck, was a coal miner, not knowing he was a railroad man who also breathed in coal dust thick and heavy. Since he did not smoke tobacco, he had to have worked for the railroad at least ten years for his lungs to reach such a condition. He followed the footsteps of his older brother Patrick, and likely began working for the railroad when he reached his early teens. He was also known to work as a gas fitter, so likely he learned the trade by working at some point for the Schenectady Gas Company located directly behind his home. Since the Hogan home was very near the railroad yards, young Michael undoubtedly began inhaling the noxious coal dust as an infant.

One thing is for certain, Hogan alias Blanck was no rube, being raised in one of the most progressive and enterprising cities in America during the last half of the nineteenth century. The town of Schenectady was founded in July, 1661, by fifteen Dutchmen who obtained deed to land from friendly Mohawk Indians. The name Schenectady was derived from the Iroquoian phrase, *Scag-nac-ta-de*, meaning "Beyond the pine plains," and has been spelled seventy-nine different ways before the present spelling was accepted. The city was chartered on March 26, 1798.

In its formative stages Schenectady was known as "Old Dorp," a Dutch term for village, and a "sleepy little canal town" after the Erie Canal was opened in 1825. In 1851 all this changed when the Schenectady Locomotive Works, later becoming the American Locomotive Company, was founded and the town emerged as one of the largest locomotive manufacturers in the country, producing engines for railroads all over the world.

On July 4, 1885, the Remington Company illuminated State Street with electricity, and on the following February 2 all the major streets of the city were electrically lighted. On May 24, 1886, Thomas Edison's Edison Machine Works was established, and six years later, through a merger, became the General Electric Company. By 1890 these massive industrial changes earned Schenectady the title of "The city that lights and hauls the world."[4]

Michael Hogan, Jr. not only eye-witnessed these enterprising developments, but also gained proficiency as a skilled railroad workman through them. He also became an expert in the art of rough and tumble fighting, but apparently committed no crimes in

View of the Erie Canal from State Street in Schenectady, New York around the time Tom Blanck left his hometown. Blanck's house was only a few blocks west of the canal. *Courtesy Schenectady Public Library, Schenectady, New York.*

Schenectady, at least none he was charged with, for the local newspapers reported that the police had no record of him. In his confession as Tom Blanck, he stated he was from Schenectady and that his mother still lived there. Seattle's *Post-Intelligencer* inferred that he received an inferior upbringing based upon this remark by him, "Do you suppose my mother would bring me cakes and pies if she knew where I am. Oh, no, she would get an ax and come up here and kill me." An article in the *Portland Oregonian*, quoted in the March 25, 1895 issue of the *Post-Intelligencer*, undoubtedly was right on target when it reported the following: "The inevitable conclusion is that the instincts of outlawry were born with the man, and that his constant effort was in the direction of fostering them. From the time at which the public became aware of his existence he fiercely resisted all restraint, and it is but a logical conclusion that he had a stormy, wayward and ungoverned boyhood."

Hogan a.k.a. Blanck never mentioned his father, who was still living and working in Schenectady in 1895. Reading between the lines this suggests that the two were not on good terms, likely stemming from the younger Hogan's violent nature and penchant for stealing. This was the probable reason the soon-to-be killer headed west at age eighteen.[5]

[1] For the most comprehensive biography of Harry Tracy, see Jim Dullenty's *Harry Tracy: The Last Desperado.*

[2] *Seattle Post-Intelligencer*, March 29, 1895.

[3] *Evening Star* (Schenectady, New York), March 23, 1895; 1870 City of Schenectady, New York census, 5th Ward, family dwelling # 238; 1880 City of Schenectady, New York census, Schedule 1, B, p.2; 1900 City of Schenectady, New York census, Enumeration District 136, p.4; *Schenectady City Directories*, 1857–58, 1860 through 1868, 1869–70, p.44, 1875–76, p.67, 1880, p.58, 1887, p.74, 1890, p.79; *City Atlas of Schenectady, New York* (1880); *The Church Of Saint John The Baptist*, Schenectady, New York, One Hundred and Fiftieth Anniversary, 1830–1980, npn; Naturalization Petition No. 748, Michael Hogan; Baptismal Record, Michael Hogan, Jr.

[4] *Seattle Post-Intelligencer*, October 6, 1894, March 22, 1895; 1880 City of Schenectady, New York census, Schedule 1, B, p.2. The census showed that Michael Hogan was age nine and attending school; *Atlas of the City of Schenectady, New York* (1905); J. H. French, *Historical and Statistical Gazetteer of New York State*, pp.595–96, 598–99; *Schenectady...Facts and Stuff*, Prepared by Larry Hart, Schenectady County-City Historian, npn; *Important Dates in the History of Schenectady*, npn; Interview with Dr. Carl R. Nordstrom, M.D., Appalachian State University, Boone, North Carolina, May 8, 1992.

[5] *Evening Star,* March 23, 1895; *Daily Union* (Schenectady, New York), March 26, 30, 1895; *Seattle Post-Intelligencer*, March 23, 25, 1895; *Schenectady City Directory*, 1895, p.100.

CHAPTER TWO

"I Am Shot"

Around mid-1889, Michael Hogan, Jr. left New York and headed west. He apparently went to work for the Oregon Short Line Railroad where he was known to railroad employees and others along the line as Slim Jim, a nickname that he would continue to use during this period in his life. According to Charles D. King of Olympia, Washington, who had been Assistant District Attorney in Washington County, Idaho, in 1889 and 1890, Hogan teamed up with a slick and dapper thirty-year-old confidence man named James "Doc" Sweeney in southern Oregon. On March 6, 1890, Slim Jim, Sweeney and another confidence man named J. M. "Tex" Tate, took the train from Huntington, Oregon, to Weiser, Idaho.

That evening the three sharpers went to the Red Front Saloon where Tate and Sweeney began playing poker with two local citizens. Slim Jim, dressed in ranching clothes, sat at the bar playing the rustic rube, acting as if he had no connection with the other two con men. Apparently, his actions while conversing with tavern owner Johnson aroused suspicion. When the game broke up around midnight, Slim Jim commented about not being able to get up a decent poker game in Weiser. Probate Judge N. M. Hanthorn, a bystander, remarked that the saloon patrons knew the three were confidence men and started poking fun at Slim Jim's clothes.

Slim Jim's volcanic temper erupted, and he pulled a double-action .44-calibre revolver and let fly at Hanthorn. The bullet passed through the judge's coat and hit Sweeney in the right side. Slim Jim's dying partner exclaimed, "I am shot!" and fell dead on the saloon floor. Emptying his revolver at the frightened crowd, the killer fled through the back door and disappeared, losing his hat in his escape.

Sheriff Pence was not in town, so District Attorney H. S. King and his brother Charles conducted the investigation. Local officers searched the town and surrounding countryside, but to no avail. On May 7, a young boy found the murder weapon on top of an old shed back of a blacksmith shop. It contained five empty chambers and one loaded shell that had misfired. With dry humor, the *Weiser Leader* commented, "The owner can have his property by appearing and making due proof thereof."

Charles King said the killer was around twenty-one-years-old, smooth faced and well built. The *Weiser Leader* of March 14 gave this description of the killer, "Is a man about five feet 8 or 9 inches in height, and will weigh about 190 pounds. Is of light complexion, and has a smooth, full face; also has blue tattoo marks on the right wrist..." This closely matches the characteristics of Tom Blanck. In 1895, Charles King identified the body of Tom Blanck as that of the Weiser killer. Nineteen-year-old Mike Hogan had killed his first man.[1]

Undoubtedly fear of capture or retribution spurred young Hogan to flee, so he headed for the to the safety of his parents' home in Schenectady, where he boarded for a few months. By September he regained his confidence, adopted his old alias of Slim Jim and again headed west, this time for Fairhaven (now part of Bellingham), Washington.

During the early part of October several petty thefts were reported from lodging houses and private rooms throughout Fairhaven. On October 9, two suits of clothing, a pistol and some minor articles were pilfered from a cabin in Happy Valley, and the police alerted second-hand dealers to be on the lookout for the stolen goods. The next evening Slim Jim entered Howe's store on Harris Street and tried to sell one of the stolen suits of clothing. Howe stepped to the rear of his store and told another man to go for the police. The wary thief then left the store and Howe went to the home of Officer Peter Bruhn, explaining the circumstances. Bruhn quickly dressed and hurried to Harris Street where he spotted the thief leaving another store where he had disposed of his plunder.

Following his quarry to Tenth and Harris Streets, Bruhn had no trouble in arresting the thief. Within a block, the prisoner suddenly whipped out a revolver and cold-bloodedly shot Bruhn twice, one shot ricocheted off the policeman's watch and the other entered his side, glanced off a rib, and lodged under his shoulder blade. As he fell, Bruhn called for help from a gathering crowd. Several started in pursuit of the shooter, who turned, fired at his pursuers and easily disappeared into the darkness. A posse quickly formed but the fugitive made good his escape. Bruhn was fortunate, suffering only a minor wound, and he was back on duty within a few days.[2]

In a later interview in the *Post-Intelligencer*, Bruhn stated that shortly after the shooting he arrested a man for petty larceny who, for leniency, told the policeman that the shooter was Slim Jim and could be found in Port Townsend.[3]

Word was dispatched to the Port Townsend police, and Slim Jim met his match in the personage of Chief of Police Thomas R. Delaney. A powerful man of over six feet, Tom Delaney was a veteran of both gun battles and confrontations with criminals.[4] Although the *Weekly Leader* in Port Townsend gave no account of this incident, the *Seattle Post-Intelligencer* reported: "A short time after the Peter Bruhn incident at Fairhaven Delaney was after a pickpocket and arrested Tom Blanck, who was traveling at that time as James Moore. When the chief attempted to make the arrest Blanck drew his gun, but Delaney was too quick for him and had his own against the desperado's body before he could shoot. After this Blanck was mild as a kitten."[5]

In 1904, Tom Delaney was Seattle's Chief of Police, and he gave a local newspaper an account of the arrest. Although there are errors, Delaney's statement is more detailed:

> I was marshal [also Chief of Police] of Port Townsend and got word that Peter Brown [Bruhn], chief of police [policeman] at Fairhaven, was shot down by a robber. Blanck came to Townsend and stayed at a hotel kept by Mrs. Walker. She told me of his presence, as he seemed to be a questionable character, and I looked him up.
>
> Blanck was with another fellow at the time. I stopped him, and he reached for his gun. He got it almost, but I beat him to it, and he did what I told him. He gave his name as James Moore. All he had on his person besides his gun was a switch key.
>
> Yes, it was a big gun. It was a 44-caliber. It looked about 50-cal-

iber to me at the time. That's all there is to it. The Whatcom county sheriff came and got Blanck and took him back for trial, but he escaped a short time later.[6]

Policeman Peter Bruhn claimed he was sent to Port Townsend where he took custody of the fugitive and then headed back to Fairhaven by steamer. At Anacortes the prisoner, who said his name was Thomas Moore, asked to be taken off the boat to walk on the wharf. When Bruhn refused his request, Slim Jim jumped off the boat, struck his head on the railing and was easily recaptured. After two days in the Fairhaven jail, Slim Jim escaped by sawing through the bars. Where he got the tool is unknown, but undoubtedly he was savvy enough to have hidden it in his shoe or boot, banking on the premise that the lawmen and jailors would not thoroughly search him. This portion of the story, however, was never reported in the Bellingham, Fairhaven or Port Townsend newspapers. When Tom Blanck was in jail in Seattle in 1894, Bruhn visited the jail, conversed with Blanck in front of the jailer, thus proving that Blanck and Slim Jim were the same man.[7]

According to Tom Blanck, he headed for British Columbia where, in January, 1891, he robbed a stagecoach and killed the driver. A search of the records in the Spokane, Washington Public Library, the National Archives of Canada in Ottawa, the David Thompson Library in Nelson, British Columbia, and the British Columbia Archives and Records Service in Victoria failed to uncover any information on this stage robbery. However, Blanck's confession to a fellow inmate in the Seattle jail has proven to be accurate except for this incident. On the other hand, he may have been blowing smoke as stage robbery does not fit his pattern of crime. For what it is worth, here is the story quoted in both the *Seattle PostIntelligencer* and the *Vancouver Daily World*:

> He had a partner with him, but did not mention his name. While in British Columbia he learned, he said, that there were gold mines in the Kootenay region, and that Chinamen came down in stages frequently with large amounts of gold. With the "yellow boys" in view, they located in the country and soon were well acquainted with the roads and trails that came from the mines. One day they saw a stagecoach with a white driver and two

Chinamen for passengers coming down the hill, so they decided to hold them up.

The ever familiar but worn out cry "hands up" was given, but the driver showed fight and was immediately shot dead. His slayers had no idea who their victim was and made no effort to find out, but got down to business and, after scaring the Chinamen almost to death, overhauled the stage for booty. Blanck claimed that they got $3,000 in gold and $1,300 in silver. The latter was too heavy to carry, so they buried it, and, if his story is true, it has never been disturbed.

After the job was done they divided the gold and separated. Blanck returning to his home and his partner striking out for himself. They had no trouble in escaping and were not brought in contact with any officers.[8]

Although this portion of Blanck's confession is conflicting, there is proof that he did not go to Schenectady following the stage robbery. Blanck also stated that in February he went back to Washington where he committed several petty crimes. In Ellensburg, he "stuck up" a man but got nothing for his trouble. In Kalama he committed a burglary, got caught and was jailed. After a week behind bars he managed to escape and went to Wooley and "put up a job to crack Bingham and Holbrook's Bank." He got into the bank through the transom of a side door. Without tools, he relied on his skill in finding the combination to the safe. When this failed, he stole a Smith and Wesson revolver and fled from the bank. The *Seattle Post-Intelligencer* gave confirmation to this part of Blanck's confession, "Proof can be brought, however, that an attempt was made to break Bingham & Holbrook's bank at Wooley...." The article continued: "Blanck came to the conclusion that, as he was not having very good success in Washington, he would go down to California, a state he thought would be good for hold-up work. He was successful, he said, in several small pieces of work and finally went home."[9]

His escapades would continue in his home state of New York, and they aptly earned him the nickname of "Crazy Mike."

[1] *Weiser Leader*, March 14, May 9, 1890; *Seattle Post-Intelligencer*, March 25, 1895.

[2] *Schenectady City Directory*, 1890, p.79: Michael Hogan, Jr. was not listed in the 1891 *Schenectady City Directory*; *Bellingham Bay Express*, October 11, 1890; *The Weekly World* (Fairhaven, Washington), October 11, 1890.

[3] *Seattle Post-Intelligencer*, March 22, 1895.

[4] *The Weekly Leader* (Port Townsend, Washington), January 8, 1891.

[5] *Seattle Post-Intelligencer*, March 25, 1895.

[6] Unidentified Seattle newspaper article, 1904. C. B. Bagley Scrapbook, Vol. 4, p.54.

[7] *Seattle Post-Intelligencer*, March 21, 22, 1895.

[8] *Seattle Post-Intelligencer*, March 23, 1895; *Vancouver Daily World*, March 25, 1895; A search of the holdings of the Spokane Public Library, Spokane, Washington, the David Thompson Library, Nelson, British Columbia, the National Archives of Canada, Ottawa, Ontario, and the British Columbia Archives and Records Service, Victoria, British Columbia, failed to uncover any record of this stage holdup.

[9] *Seattle Post-Intelligencer*, March 23, 1895; no record of these incidents were reported in the *Kalama Bulletin*, *Weekly Leader* or the *Weekly World*.

CHAPTER THREE

Crazy Mike

Following the death of Tom Blanck, the *Post-Intelligencer* gave this report that sheds some light on his adroitness in street brawling after his return to New York:

> The latest information concerning Blanck's record is that he lived at one time in Amsterdam, N.Y., and was known as "Crazy Mike." By trade he was a gas fitter, but about half of the time he worked on the New York & Erie Railroad as a brakeman.
>
> In all the country around there was no one who wanted to engage with him in a rough and tumble fight, for he had "done up" six or seven people. So far as is known, however, he was never at that period guilty of taking life. The man who gave this information is a Mr. Spencer, of Portland, Or., and he positively identified the remains yesterday. The story comes from a source the reliability of which cannot be doubted.[1]

After two years in New York, Crazy Mike Hogan headed west again. According to Seattle resident Fred Bouchard, Hogan was in San Francisco, California, during the summer of 1893, and was using the alias of James H. Brown. Bouchard stated he met the man-killer in San Francisco and, in 1895, this report was written in the *Post-Intelligencer* after he had identified Blanck's body as Brown:

> The moment he [Bouchard] saw the features of the dead despera-do he recognized him as James H. Brown, whom he saw in San Francisco about two years ago. He was then stopping at the Western hotel with Bouchard, and as both stopped there for a long

time Bouchard came to know him.... While at the Western Brown never talked much to any one, and seemed to keep to himself, so that he made no acquaintances. He dressed well but not like a laboring man, and Bouchard could not say what his business could have been. Bouchard stayed one whole summer at the Western and during that time Blanck came there several times, remaining a few weeks at a time.

From Bouchard's observations, Blanck apparently was free-lancing as a petty crook or burglar in San Francisco.[2]

In the fall of 1893, Blanck headed for Houston, Texas. Former Lake Shore Railroad conductor G. W. Regan, who also identified Blanck's body in Seattle, stated to the *Post-Intelligencer* that in November, 1893, the desperado went to work for the Houston and Texas Central Railroad and served under him as head brakeman on freight train no. 4. Regan said that he was known in Texas as Thomas Hamilton Blanck, and gave the names and addresses of the Superintendent and the Road Master of the railroad to corroborate his story. Ironically, the conductor gave the newspaper a much different view of Blanck's character, stating "He was one of the most kind hearted, free, generous men that ever worked on the road and would give his last nickel to a friend."

Regan also related accounts of Blanck's prowess with his fists and his gun: "In talking of Blanck, Regan said he was a great fighter and once in Houston saw him lick three men alone. At another time he saw him empty his revolver at freight car No. 123 at forty paces distance. Blanck put every bullet in the lower ring of the figure 5."[3]

During a short period of the time when Blanck was supposed to be in Texas, the *Seattle Post-Intelligencer* and the *Daily Union* in Schenectady, New York, credited him with two murders committed in Montana. The *Daily Union* reported, "Supposed murders not included in his confession: James Skinner, station agent at Great Belgrade, Mont. [sic: W. H. Ogle; Skinner was killed in Culbertson, Montana by Frank Robinson who was arrested and jailed in February, 1894]; Policeman John Flynn, at Helena, Mont." Regan did not mention Blanck's absence from Texas; however, he was never asked this question. In his confession, without realizing the implications, Blanck admitted that he was in Montana at the time of these killings and stated he was there for three weeks, almost the exact time span of the killings. He also said that he killed a lawman, but did not give details. Flynn was the only law officer killed in the area where Blanck was known to be.[4]

These murders were typical of Blanck's other killings, and it is probable that he committed them. Further evidence against Blanck came from a man from Missoula, who saw the killer in the King County jail, and stated that he saw Blanck in his city about the time these crimes were committed. A probable scenario is that during his trips to and from the West Coast Blanck passed through Montana and decided to return and pull a few robberies. Taking leave from his Texas job around the first of April, 1894, Blanck headed for Montana. Since Blanck was a railroad man, he likely took a job with the Northern Pacific and worked out of Missoula, committing the crimes when he reached each of the two towns. He later stated he had worked for the Northern Pacific, but the complete time frame is unclear. Both crimes were committed at a Northern Pacific depot, which is also incriminating.

In the early morning hours of April 10, 1894, a burglar picked the lock of the Saltzgaber and Sellers blacksmith shop in Helena, Montana, and stole a sledgehammer, a brace and some chisels, and then headed for the Northern Pacific depot. Picking the lock of the waiting room door around 3:00 a.m., the thief entered the depot, picked another door lock and proceeded to the lighted ticket office where the safe was kept. Prying open the office door, the burglar began drilling into the safe above the handle. Not much cash was normally kept in the safe, but it was surmised that the burglar knew that ticket agent A. B. Avery had placed $135 in the safe that day.

At 3:15 a.m., forty-five-year-old John W. Flynn, a six-year veteran of the Helena police force, passed Twohy's Saloon, briefly spoke with janitor Thomas Breslin, and walked off toward the depot. Needing to use the toilet, Flynn entered the depot, heard noises coming from the ticket office and walked toward the open doorway.

The thief apparently heard Flynn's footsteps, and when the policeman reached the door he swung the chisel at his head, knocking him down with glancing blow. Flynn was armed with two pistols, one in his coat and another in his back pocket. As Flynn attempted to rise and draw the revolver from his coat, the burglar cut loose with his .44 and fired five shots. Two slugs plowed into the floor near the downed policeman, but three hit the officer, one in left leg above the knee and another into the top of his left shoulder, which ranged downward into his chest. The third and fatal bullet entered the top of his head and lodged in his mouth. Flynn was dead before his body hit the floor.

In panic, the murderer apparently took Flynn's pistol and fled from the building into the darkness, leaving his tools behind. Janitor Louis Barso found the body at 5:15 a.m. and immediately informed the police. During the investigation police officers interviewed several witnesses who claimed to have heard the shots but saw nothing. The murder remained unsolved.[5]

At 1:05 a.m. on April 26, an alarm went off in the home of Northern Pacific Station Agent W. H. Ogle in Belgrade, Montana. The alarm had been rigged from the safe in the depot office to the bedroom of Ogle's home just across the railroad tracks. Springing from his bed, Ogle dressed hurriedly and grabbed his gun. Ignoring the pleas from his wife not to go, Ogle assured her he would be careful and dashed off into the rainy night toward the depot office.

Reaching the office, Ogle peered into the window and was greeted with three shots from a .44-calibre revolver. One bullet missed Ogle, the second entered the left side of his chest and ranged downward, and the third struck his right wrist before plowing into his right side. His assailant was so close that the agent's face was powder-burned. Ogle's wife heard the shots but was so paralyzed with fear that she waited until 5:00 a.m. before she went to the depot. She discovered her husband's body on the depot platform with his cocked revolver beside his hand.

The *Helena Weekly Herald* reported, "The circumstances are so nearly like those surrounding the murder of Policeman Flynn at Helena that it is supposed the deed was done by the same man." Apparently lying low until the heat from the Flynn murder died down, the killer had waited sixteen days before pulling this job at Belgrade, twelve miles west of Bozeman. He again stole tools from a blacksmith shop and forced open the door of the depot. When he started to work on the safe he was unaware of the alarm going off, but he evidently heard Ogle's footsteps on the platform and fired three close range shots from the doorway at the stooping agent.

Again, leaving the tools behind, the killer fled from the depot and disappeared. The safe was left untouched.

Sheriff Caldwell and his deputies from Gallatin County, ex-Deputy Marshal Jackson, Under-Sheriff Hoss of Lewis and Clarke County, and Detective Walters of Helena, conducted a widespread search and investigation. As in the Helena murder, no clues were discovered and the murderer remained at large.[6]

Blanck undoubtedly felt the heat generated by the killings and quickly made tracks back to Texas, resuming his job on the railroad. And it was not until a year later, in Seattle, that these two murders were charged to him. Conductor G. W. Regan reported that three months later he and Tom Blanck left Texas together for Portland, Oregon, arriving there in early August, 1894. Here the two men separated with Regan going to Mexico City. Blanck headed for Montana and launched another murderous rampage; his previous violent acts being only preliminaries to the main event.[7]

[1] *Seattle Post-Intelligencer*, March 24, 1895.

[2] *Seattle Post-Intelligencer*, March 22, 1895.

[3] *Seattle Post-Intelligencer*, March 23, 1895.

[4] *Daily Union*, March 30, 1895; *Seattle Post-Intelligencer*, March 23, 1895; *Helena Weekly Herald*, February 22, 1894.

[5] *Seattle Post-Intelligencer*, October 6, 1894; *Helena Weekly Herald*, April 19, 1894.

[6] *Helena Weekly Herald*, May 3, 1894; *Avant Courier* (Bozeman, Montana), April 28, 1894.

[7] *Seattle Post-Intelligencer*, March 23, 1895.

CHAPTER FOUR

A Fiend from Hell

The *Helena Daily Herald* chronicled Tom Blanck's arrival in Montana with this graphic statement, "The 'tough' characters who always appear in Montana during the racing season made their debut in Helena yesterday." The newspaper was referring to Blanck's three hold-ups that occurred on August 17, 1894.

At 2:10 a.m. Freight Conductor Straub arrived at the Northern Pacific depot at Helena in charge of an extra train brought in from Missoula. Straub, receiving orders to take another freight train west to Elliston at 2:30, went into the yards to check out the train. Engrossed in his work, the conductor was suddenly confronted by Tom Blanck, who shoved a .45-calibre revolver under his nose and ordered him to put his hands up. Straub immediately complied, and the masked bandit then told him to hand over his money, which came to a paltry $2.50. The small haul angered Blanck, and he demanded the conductor's watch. Straub refused and began to argue with the robber just as another engine appeared, washing the area with its glaring headlight.

With a curse Tom Blanck took a backwards step, aimed his revolver, shot the hapless conductor in the thigh and disappeared into the darkness. The wound proved to be minor, and with Blanck's known proficiency as a marksman, it appears that his intent was not to kill the conductor but to give him a little pay back for his defiance. Because of the excitement and confusion caused by the robbery, an hour passed before anyone thought to inform the police.

Shortly after ten o'clock that evening business had slacked off at the prestigious Hotel Broadwater in Helena, and bartender Billy Friend stepped out on the porch at the rear of the bar to get some fresh air. From out of the darkness Tom Blanck, unmasked and

Artist's sketch made in 1894 of the Broadwater Hotel in Helena, Montana. *Courtesy Montana Historical Society, Helena*

dressed in overalls, approached Friend and handed him a tin can. Thinking the man wanted a drink, Friend headed for the bar and asked what he wanted. Blanck curtly replied, "Put the money in it." "Oh, you're joking," the bartender quipped. "No, I'm not," replied Blanck as Friend turned and saw a revolver leveled at him.

As the bartender's hands shot upward, tin can and all, hotel manager C. B. Garrett and Burton Hall entered the bar from the billiard hall. "What's the matter, Billy?" asked Garrett. And when the frightened bartender nodded his head in the direction of the robber, the two men quickly raised their hands in unison. Ordering his captives to get in line, Blanck hustled them behind the bar, rang up "change" on the cash register and removed $100. During the action, two hotel guests entered the bar, saw what was happening and imitated the others by throwing their hands in the air.

Blanck coolly told his victims that the state of their health depended upon them remaining in this position until he was long gone. Heeding the robber's warning, they watched him back out of the open door, vault over the porch railing and disappear. The victims claimed that the robber had an accomplice on guard outside the bar.

As soon as it was safe, Garrett telephoned the sheriff's office. By chance, Police Sergeant Murphy entered the hotel shortly after the robbery and telephoned the news to his headquarters. Within an hour of the robbery, Sheriff Curtis and Under-Sheriff Hoss had officers spread out over the area in search of the hold-up man. The next morning the police arrested a one-armed man in a saloon, thinking him to be Blanck's partner, but Garrett and others said he was not the wanted man.[1]

Leaving the grounds of the Broadwater, Tom Blanck hurried a few hundred yards east to the Palace Billiard Hall where he encountered bartender Richard Bolt standing in the doorway. Never one to miss an opportunity, Blanck demanded the contents of the till. Bolt refused, and as he jumped back into the hall the robber pulled his gun, pushed through the doorway and ordered the bartender to go behind the bar and bring him the money.

When Bolt reached the end of the bar where Blanck was standing, the gutsy bartender jumped him. The *Helena Independent* reported:

A struggle followed for the gun, but as Bolt is only a small man and the other fellow was of pretty good weight, the plucky bartender could not keep his hold, and the robber broke away. Although he retained possession of the gun he made no attempt to use it, but ran out the door as fast as he could in the direction of the city, evidently having had enough of the nervy little bartender.

In the struggle over the gun the robber's black slouch hat fell off, and he did not take time to pick it up when he finished his interview with Bolt.[2]

Tom Blanck was never one to run from a fight, and it was likely fear of being caught for the Broadwater robbery that made him flee. In Blanck's confession to a fellow prisoner in Seattle, he said his partner weakened and ran away. Leaving the Broadwater, Blanck ran a mile and a half. Feeling safe, he proceeded to rob a poor man, forcing him to give up his hat and exchange trousers.

Noting the shabby condition of his victim, Blanck took pity on him and gave him twelve dollars from the Broadwater take. The desertion of his partner enraged Blanck, and he set out to kill him. When his anger cooled, he gave up this idea and decided to rob another saloon.[3]

Picking up a more reliable confederate, Blanck entered the Atlantic beer hall shortly after 1:00 a.m., Sunday, September 2. While his masked cohort covered the twenty-some patrons from the doorway with his revolver, Blanck, who was also masked, moved along the bar and ordered everyone to put their hands up. Leveling his revolver at bartender Henry Wolff, Blanck walked behind the bar, opened the cash register and scooped up the cash. He then asked Wolff how much money he had. Receiving the curt reply, "Nothing," Blanck thrust his hand into the bartender's pocket and removed the month's wages he had just received. With a take of $300, both robbers backed out of the bar and boldly walked down Main Street. Deeming it safe, the customers ran to the doorway just in time to see the hold-up men disappear up Lawrence Street. Although the police quickly began a widespread search, the two robbers safely made their getaway.[4]

Tom Blanck likely figured he had worn out his welcome in Helena and headed south for Butte. The next crime credited to him and his unnamed partner occurred on the night of September 6. Major Camp (it is unknown if Major was a title or an actual first name) was walking home on Alaska Street about 11:00 p.m. when two men accosted him. While his partner stood in the shade in an alley, Blanck, wearing a slouch hat and brandishing a revolver, ordered Camp to throw up his hands. Instead of complying, Camp bravely struck the pistol arm of the robber with his walking stick while calling out loudly for the police. The hot-headed Blanck aimed his revolver at the major's head and pulled the trigger, but the gun misfired. As his screaming victim backed up, the gunman continued to snap the misfiring pistol. From the shadows the partner made a remark to the incensed robber and fled up the alley. Cursing the man, Blanck swung his revolver at Camp's head but the blow was warded off. The robber then took off running towards the Gaguon mine and made his escape. The next night Blanck struck again, this time with deadly results.[5]

At 11:00 p.m. in Meaderville, just north of Butte, the front door of the Primavero and Grosso Saloon swung open revealing two masked gunmen. The twenty-four patrons froze as the larger robber, wearing worn-out shoes with no heels, approached co-owner Steve Grosso with his revolver leveled. As the other hold-up man covered the crowd with two pistols, Blanck told everyone to raise their hands and warned them, "Don't move. If you do, you are dead men."

Ordering Grosso to get the cash, Blanck followed him behind the bar and emptied the contents of the cash drawer into a sack tied around his waist. "Is this all the money you got?" the robber questioned, and when Grosso said yes, Blanck made the barman turn his back while he ransacked the drawers in the back bar. Turning to Grosso, the robber took his watch, went through his pockets and then took an expensive bottle of whiskey from the shelf. The booty amounted to $150 in cash and Grosso's watch worth $150. Cautioning Grosso not to move for five minutes, Blanck joined his partner at the door.

At this juncture, co-owner Joe Primavero and a patron made a break for the side door and escaped while Grosso grabbed a revolver from behind the bar. The robbers shouted for him to drop the weapon and Blanck opened fire. Grosso got off one shot before he was hit. Blanck's shot passed through the bartender's right arm between his shoulder and elbow, struck the seventh rib and penetrated his lung. Grosso exclaimed that he was a dead man and sat down in a chair. He died the next morning at 11:20.

Leaving the saloon, one of the robbers repeated, "Don't move. If you do, you are dead men." The escaped customer ran to the Vienna Saloon and told Antone Donati, day jailer at the county jail, that the saloon was being robbed. Securing a revolver, Donati ran toward the saloon and spotted the two bandits running down the street. When the jailer ordered the two men to stop, Blanck replied, "Stop nothing," and fired two shots at Donati, one grazing his cheek. Donati opened fire but missed the fleeing robbers, who split up, one heading north and the other south into the darkness.

From Grosso's saloon, Donati telephoned for a physician and notified the sheriff's office. Through the night and into the next evening Sheriff Reynolds, Under-Sheriff Young and number of deputies vainly searched for the fugitives. The *Daily Inter Mountain* stated that the robbers were likely aware it was payday at the mines, and that they were pros who skillfully covered their tracks. Blanck had been noticed around 9:30 p.m. in Martin Stephens' saloon in Meaderville wearing the heelless shoes. The only evidence ever uncovered was the stolen bottle of whiskey found by an officer in a gopher hole at the Boston and Montana smelter.[6]

The shooting of Grosso put Blanck and his confederate on the run, and they headed for Marysville, about fifty miles to the north. Around 2:00 a.m. on September 13, they pulled another robbery. Everything was closing down in the Club Saloon; co-proprietor Howard Irwin and his brother John were tallying the daily receipts, faro dealer Joe Garrett was closing the game, bartender John Duffy was dozing in a chair and a dozen customers were shooting the breeze when the two armed men entered the door with the familiar command, "Hands up, everybody."

John Irwin had a $600 roll of bills in his hand and hesitated, stuffing the bills inside his hat. "Keep your hands up," snarled Blanck, and Irwin quickly raised his empty hands. "Faces to the wall," ordered the robbers, and Blanck went through the victim's pockets, taking a gold watch from Duffy and cash from everyone. One man with only forty-five cents was allowed to keep his money.

Sticking his revolver under the bartender's nose, Blanck forced him to point out one of the proprietors, Charles Peabody, who was ordered to open the safe. Blanck put the cash drawer under his arm and walked to the doorway. With a parting command to stay inside, the two robbers disappeared into the night with $175, missing the money in Irwin's hat and another $500 in a separate part of the safe. One of the patrons ran to the door with a rifle and fired four ineffectual shots at the fleeing bandits.

Sheriff Curtis and Under-Sheriff Hoss came up from Helena, and, together with Constable Hendricks, searched the area unsuccessfully for two days. Sending telegrams to officials throughout the area, the lawmen concluded they were the same men who robbed the Broadwater and that they had escaped into the mountains south of Marysville. Unknown to the lawmen, both robbers were close by in a miner's cabin where Blanck would commit the most depraved crime of his sordid career.[7]

From Marysville, the two desperados had fled to the nearby mining area of Skelley's Gulch where, in typical western style, they were given food and shelter by miner John Randolph and his partner. After several days Blanck and his cohort left and reportedly took shelter in an abandoned cabin.

Early on the morning of September 19, Randolph's partner went to their diggings while Randolph remained at the cabin to finish some chores. Suddenly two masked men entered the cabin, seized the miner around the neck and threw him to the floor. When Randolph resisted and yelled for his partner, his two assailants choked and bound him and then demanded his money and gold.

Randolph told them there was no money, that it was deposited in a bank in Helena. Doubting his statement the two robbers built a fire in the stove and thrust two pieces of scrap iron into the fire until they were red hot. Stuffing a towel in the miner's mouth, they brutally applied the hot irons to his bare right leg. Removing the towel, they again asked where the money was and received the same reply from their hapless victim.

The *Helena Daily Herald* graphically described what followed:

> Then the fiends of hell heated the iron again, and then, despite his struggles, forced it into his right ear, where it made a terrible burn. They then chloroformed their victim and ransacked the place, stealing a watch and rifle, and leaving Randolph unconscious struck into the hills.

> A few minutes later Randolph's partner went to see what had become of his working mate, finding him bound and unconscious and horribly burned. He received immediate attention and will soon be around again.

Randolph reported that during the initial struggle the mask of one of the robbers was dislodged and he recognized him as one of the men that he had sheltered. From his description there was no doubt that they were the same men who robbed the Club Saloon. The Helena police found no trace of the two robbers.[8]

Of all these crimes, Blanck later admitted to the robberies of the Broadwater in Helena and the Club Saloon in Marysville. He also confessed to the murders of Steve Grosso and an unnamed lawman (presumably John Flynn), but due to the senseless torture of John Randolph, he likely chose to forget that one.

In lieu of the torment inflicted upon John Randolph, Tom

Blanck knew that if he was caught in Montana he could expect no less than a necktie party. Blanck would later state to Police Chief Bolton Rogers following his capture in Seattle that after splitting with his partner, he worked along the line of the Northern Pacific until he reached Tacoma, Washington. Here, the killer would launch another bloody spree.[9]

[1] *Helena Daily Herald*, August 18, 1894; *The Daily Independent*, August 18, 1894.

[2] *Helena Independent*, August 19, 1894.

[3] *Seattle Post-Intelligencer*, March 23, 1895.

[4] *Helena Daily Herald*, September 4, 1894; *Marysville Gazette*, September 6, 1894.

[5] *Daily Inter Mountain* (Butte, Montana), September 7, 1894.

[6] *Daily Inter Mountain*, September 8, 10, 13, 1894; *Helena Daily Herald*, September 10, 1894.

[7] *The Mountaineer* (Marysville, Montana), September 20, 1894; *Marysville Gazette*, September 20, 1894.

[8] *Helena Daily Herald*, September 21, 1894; *The Mountaineer*, September 27, 1894; *Marysville Gazette*, September 27, 1894.

[9] *Seattle Post-Intelligencer*, October 5, 6, 1894.

CHAPTER FIVE

"That's What I Shot For"

Tom Blanck arrived in Tacoma around September 25 and took lodging at the Appleton House on Pacific Avenue managed by a Mrs. Earle. The killer paid in advance for room and board, then feigned sickness and was fed and sheltered by his landlady for a couple of days. She also furnished him with clothing.[1]

Also on September 25, John Brooks, age twenty-eight, serving eight months for smuggling, escaped from the U. S. Penitentiary on McNeil's Island. According to the *Post-Intelligencer*, Blanck and Brooks were members of both a gang of professional crooks headquartered at Missoula, Montana, and a band of smugglers in Washington.[2]

One of the most lucrative criminal enterprises in Washington in the 1890s was smuggling due to the proximity of the Canadian border. Excerpted from the story of smuggler Jake Terry in the author's book, *Tales Never Told Around The Campfire*:

From the late 1880s through the early 1900s, smuggling illegal Chinese aliens and opium across the Canadian border into Washington was a lucrative enterprise. Beginning in 1862, the United States passed a series of Exclusion Acts limiting the entry of Chinese into the country. Because of the heavy influx of Chinese immigrants that had entered the United States to work at extremely low wages, U.S. citizens, nationally as well as in Washington, were up in arms over the situation. Residents in Washington claimed the Chinese were stopping the demand for white labor and spreading disease and vice.

Because of the pressure, the United States Congress took further action by passing the Exclusion Act of May 5, 1882. In essence this act halted any future Chinese laborers from entering the U.S. and specified that only those Chinese who had entered the United States prior to November 17, 1880 would be allowed to remain. These legal aliens were issued certificates as proof of residence. After this act was passed, the smuggling of illegal Chinese became extremely profitable and caused serious problems for the United States Customs Service. This was especially true in Washington as smuggling could be accomplished by water as well as by land. For each Chinese smuggled into the United States in 1890, the going rate was anywhere from twenty-three dollars to sixty dollars.

The other moneymaking smuggling commodity was opium. Although opium was not illegal in the United States, there were heavy duties placed on it, thus the smuggling of opium became a profitable business. The Tariff Act of 1897 placed a duty as high as six dollars per pound of smoking opium. In 1890, it was estimated that 172 illegal Chinese aliens and 1,400 pounds of opium were being smuggled into Washington every month.[3]

Apparently, through other crooks in Tacoma, Tom Blanck got word to John Brooks to meet him in that city. Following his escape from McNeil's Island, Brooks made his way to Yakima where he hopped aboard a railroad coal car occupied by a fifteen-year-old Hillsboro, Oregon, youth named Franklin "Frank" McMurray. The following is abstracted from McMurray's conflicting statements made to a reporter from the *Post-Intelligencer* after his capture a few days later. The boy never named Brooks, but said the man asked him if he had ever done anything crooked. McMurray told him he had stolen a revolver and had been put in reform school in Hillsboro, Oregon, from where he had escaped the past spring. Brooks told the youth about his schemes to rob banks and stores, and the two went to Tacoma to meet Blanck.

Arriving in Tacoma around the twenty-seventh, the two met Blanck at a saloon on Pacific Avenue. The killer was now calling himself Frank Hamilton, likely choosing the name from the street in Schenectady on which he was raised. Brooks and McMurray then

Panoramic view of Seattle, Washington in 1884. *Courtesy, Division of Archives and Records Management, Olympia, Washington.*

took lodging at Blanck's boarding house. McMurray said both men were kind to him and gave him money.

The next day Blanck bought a false beard and mustache. That evening, while the three criminals were walking along a Tacoma street, Brooks pulled a gun on a man and woman and ordered the man to put up his hands. When the man failed to obey, Brooks fired at him but missed. The man quickly raised his hands. During the robbery McMurray said Blanck turned and ran, but added, "I am sure, however, that Hamilton is not afraid of a dozen men, for after he shoots he is as cool as if he was shooting for practice." This statement came from first-hand knowledge when the boy witnessed Blanck's homicidal tendencies a few days later. On the twenty-ninth, Brooks left Blanck and his young companion, stating that he would work his way back to Yakima and for the two to join him there.[4]

During his stay at the boarding house, Blanck lost his key. He told Mrs. Earle he had another key that would unlock the door and would give her this key when he left. Learning that Blanck planned to leave on the morning of September 30 still owing her rent money, Mrs. Earle asked him for the key. Blanck refused to give it to her and she became irate. When the woman continued to berate him, Blanck became enraged and snarled, "God Damn you, get out of this, or I will throw you over the banister." Realizing the killer was in dead earnest, Mrs. Earle wisely backed off. Blanck left with his master key.[5]

Blanck and McMurray left on foot at 9:00 a.m. and headed for Puyallup, ten miles southeast of Tacoma. McMurray graphically described Blanck's proficiency with a revolver: "On the way Hamilton showed me what he could do with his revolver. He wore it in a holster at his side, and without making a false motion would grab it, pull it out, twirl it on his finger and come into shooting position with the gun cocked....He would twirl the gun and without apparently taking aim, hit any small object within pistol shot distance. The cleverest thing he did was to knock the center out of a dime at thirty feet. He put it in a split stick, which he stuck in the ground, and then drawing his gun from his holster brought it down and instantly fired. The dime was hit in the center."

Arriving at Meeker, a train stop at Puyallup, the two put their bundle behind a lumber office and ate a midday meal at Scott's Hotel. In the late afternoon they grabbed their bundle and hopped a train. Realizing the train was headed for Seattle they jumped off and again put their packet back of the lumber office. As they headed for the lumberyard, they spotted a man unwrapping and examining their gear. Blanck told McMurray, "Go back and tell that fellow that is our bundle." By the time McMurray reached the man, he had taken a revolver from Blanck's belongings and put it in his pocket.

According to author Thomas Duke, "Constable William Jeffrey of Puyallup, Wash., visited relatives a short distance from town, and about 5 p.m., he, in company with Thomas Alexander and Tom Bowley [sic: Boulay], was returning home on foot." Jeffrey was reportedly looking for stolen goods and opium when he pocketed Blanck's revolver. At this point Blanck walked back to the man and told him to "Drop that," referring to the revolver. "Is that yours?" questioned the constable, and Blanck answered yes. Jeffrey asked the killer if there were any identifying marks. Growing tired and

THOMAS BLANCK.

Artist's sketch of Tom Blanck, 1894, from the Seattle *Post-Intelligencer*.

impatient with this line of questioning, Blanck testily answered, "Yes, D.P.," and suddenly drew his revolver. "Hands up," ordered the killer and, before the constable could react, he shot the officer through the heart. As he fell, Jeffrey uttered his last words, "You have shot me through and through."

There were several men in the area and Blanck bolted for the brush, followed closely by McMurray. Following a lumber road, McMurray reached the railroad tracks and heard someone behind him call out, "Is that you?" Answering in the affirmative, McMurray watched Blanck nonchalantly walk up to him with his hands in his pockets.

"Did I kill that fellow?" asked Blanck.

"Yes," McMurray replied, "you put it through his heart."

"That's what I shot for," the killer coolly replied.

McMurray later stated that within a short distance they saw some men who were hunting them, and Blanck said to his young companion, "I would not turn out for one or two men; I'd kill them if they interfered, but I guess there are too many of them in that gang. I'll turn out."

With that Blanck disappeared into the brush after telling the boy he would meet him in Palmer. McMurray brazened his way through two sets of guards and headed for South Prairie, Washington, alone. It was also reported that the fugitives held up a farmer, stole his team and headed south for Orting where they split up.[6]

At first the Washington authorities believed Jeffrey's murderer was John Brooks, and Pierce County Sheriff A. C. Matthews stationed guards on all bridges and wagon roads. He ordered his deputies to take the killer dead or alive. The next morning Kittitas County Sheriff McGrath brought bloodhounds from Ellensburg, but rain rendered it impossible for the dogs to trail the fugitive.

The law officers concentrated their manhunt around South Prairie and Orting. The conductor of a train bound for Tacoma spotted McMurray near South Prairie. When the train reached Orting the information was passed to Sheriff Matthews, who in turn wired his deputies in South Prairie. Duke claimed McMurray was spotted acting suspiciously while purchasing a large amount of provisions in a store in South Prairie. Either way, the youth was immediately arrested on a road outside town, and taken to Tacoma by deputies Mark Schneider and James Knox on the three o'clock train.

Frank McMurray wasted no time in spilling his guts, but denied any involvement in Jeffrey's murder, naming Frank Hamilton as the killer. When asked why Hamilton killed the constable, McMurray replied, "Just because he wanted to do some shooting, I guess." Although it was never proved that the third man with Blanck and McMurray was John Brooks, the discovery of his jail clothing in Blanck's valise, which was found by deputies in Puyallup on October 3, provides confirmation.

Sheriff Matthews decided to concentrate his deputies around the town of McMillin. For a distance of thirty miles around the area almost every rancher was notified. Arming themselves, they too joined in the manhunt. By the evening of the second there were more than 100 officers on Blanck's trail.[7]

[1] *Seattle Post-Intelligencer*, October 5, 1894.

[2] *Seattle Post-Intelligencer*, October 2, 4, 7, 1894.

[3] Mark Dugan, *Tales Never Told Around The Campfire*, pp.129-30. Sources: Roland L. DeLorme, "The United States Bureau of Customs and Smuggling on Puget Sound, 1851 to 1913," *Prologue, Journal of The National Archives*, Summer 1973, Volume 5, Number 2, p.84; Richard W. Markov, "A Decade of Enforcement, The Chinese Exclusion And Whatcom County, 1890 to 1900," August 20, 1972, pp.1-4, 9-11.

[4] *Seattle Post-Intelligencer*, October 4, 7, 1894.

[5] *Seattle Post-Intelligencer*, October 9, 1894; *Seattle Telegraph*, October 9, 1894.

[6] *Seattle Post-Intelligencer*, October 1, 4, 7, 1894; two books concisely cover Tom Blanck's criminal career in Washington: Clarence B. Bagley, *History Of Seattle From The Earliest Settlements To The Present Time*, Volume II, pp.693-96; Thomas S. Duke, *Celebrated Criminal Cases Of America*, pp.292-95.

[7] *Seattle Post-Intelligencer*, October 1, 3, 5, 1894.

CHAPTER SIX

"I Would Kill You for Fifty Cents"

While law officers were combing the countryside for Tom Blanck, the funeral of William Jeffrey was held in Puyallup at 10:00 a.m., October 2. All the stores in town were closed, and everyone turned out for the sad event held in the Presbyterian Church. Jeffrey left a mother and wife to grieve him.

Following his split with McMurray, Tom Blanck followed the railroad tracks east for a few miles and holed up in an abandoned shack until nightfall. Resuming his trek, Blanck did what Sheriff Matthews predicted and reached the bridge spanning the Puyallup River at McMillin—he was just in time for another shootout.

Sheriff Matthews had stationed deputies Harry Moore and John Ball at the bridge on the night of the killing. Around 2:00 a.m. Moore spotted the killer and, not knowing who he was, spoke to him. Blanck reacted in his usual manner, at thirty paces he put a bullet in Moore's side and bolted for the brush. Moore was lucky; it was dark and the wound proved to be minor, a fourteen-inch gash along his side.

The next day, the manhunt shifted to the banks of the White River, twelve miles south of Buckley, when reports filtered in that the fugitive had been sighted there. Around fifty lawmen converged on the area. A false rumor also circulated that a gunfight had taken place between Blanck and law officers in the coalmining town of Burnett. When no sign of the fugitive was found by October 4, Sheriff Matthews realized the killer had escaped his net and called off the search. It was humorously reported that the bloodhounds were very good at treeing chipmunks and tracking pheasants.[1]

During the heat of the manhunt, Tom Blanck made his way along the railroad tracks to Seattle. On the afternoon of Wednesday, October 3, Blanck rented a room from Amelia Hartley, landlady of the Bay View Lodging House on the corner of West and Clay Streets in North Seattle. After paying for the room, Blanck immediately left the house.

In the evening Blanck twice cased the Mug Saloon on South Third Street and Main Street before entering the folding doors of the Third Street entrance at 10:20 p.m. The bartender, twenty-seven-year-old Charles H. Birdwell, was standing a few feet away from owner William H. Codrick, who was counting money from the cash register; Edward Reese, a relative of Codrick, was behind the bar, and six customers were sitting in the saloon. Codrick looked up and saw the robber advancing with a .45 revolver in his hand. At the command of "Hands up!" and the ominous click of the revolver's hammer, Codrick coolly replied, "Yes, my hands are up, I guess you want a drink."

Codrick was still fumbling with his cash when Blanck sprang on top of the bar and again ordered everyone to put up his hands. Patron Ed Spranger bolted for the door but froze in his tracks when Blanck growled, "Where are you going, you son of a bitch?" As he came to a quick halt, Spranger nervously jested, "I'll just trot you a heat on that," (meaning he would move quickly) and went back. Blanck just grinned. The nervy Codrick glared at the gunman and said, "I know you, and there are two men coming."

At this juncture, Birdwell muttered, "Get the gun. The guy is crazy," and whirled to grab a revolver from a drawer. Blanck cut loose. The bullet burned a gash through the top of the bar and entered the bartender's heart. Without a sound, Birdwell staggered backward and was dead before he hit the floor. By the time Codrick snatched the revolver from the drawer, Blanck had leaped from the bar and slipped out the front door to Main Street.

Policeman Gil Philbrick heard the shooting and within seconds rushed into the bar. Thinking Codrick was the guilty party, the officer pulled his gun on the owner. When the customers shouted that the murderer had fled, Philbrick flew out the door but lost the fugitive on Main Street. Five minutes later Chief of Police Bolton

Rogers had his men after the desperado. Detectives Phillips, James Wells and Ed Cudihee, Sergeant F. Willard and policemen Philbrick, Barbee, and John Corbett worked through the city without finding a trace of the killer. In the rush, Detective Wells fell down and his revolver accidentally discharged, setting his clothes on fire.

Leaving the murder scene, Blanck ran a short distance, slowed up and walked to the waterfront. He returned to his lodging house around 11:20 p.m. The next morning, news of the killing hit the papers, and Blanck's landlady read it. When Blanck awoke he shaved off his mustache and beard and feigned sickness, so Mrs. Hartley fed him. As the killer wolfed down every bite, Mrs. Hartley's son Albert murmured, "That man ain't sick and I am sure he is the man the police want." Between noon and 1 p.m., the boy rushed to the police station and reported his suspicions to Detective Cudihee.

At first Cudihee thought this was just one of the many leads he had to run down. Later that afternoon he decided to check it out and headed for the lodging house with officer John Corbett. The first act of the Tom Blanck road show was almost over.[2]

At 5:30 p.m., October 4, Cudihee walked down a path through a vacant lot leading to the lodging house with Policeman Corbett following at a distance. While Corbett concealed himself behind a pile of underbrush, Cudihee entered the hall at the rear of the house, went to the second floor and came face to face with Tom Blanck. The killer turned and immediately went into his room as Cudihee proceeded to Mrs. Hartley's room and told her, "I will have a talk with him before I go and see who he is."

Walking to the end of the hall, the detective signaled Corbett and rapped on the door at room no. 4. Blanck had the advantage, he knew when he opened the door that the man was a policeman. The room was only 8' x 10', with the bed taking up most of the space. "What do you want?" questioned the killer, and Cudihee quickly entered the room, saying, "I want to have a talk with you," and walked to the end of the bed. Blanck kicked the door closed and locked it, turned, drew a single-action Colt .45 and snarled, "Throw up your hands, you son of a bitch," as he pointed the gun at Cudihee's head.

Reacting quickly, the gutsy detective ducked his head and charged Blanck, smashing his head against the killer's. Blanck

THE MURDERED MAN.

Artist's sketch of Charles Birdwell, Tom Blanck's murder victim in Seattle, as depicted in the *Seattle Telegraph*.

pulled the trigger, but the move saved Cudihee's life. The shot grazed the detective's neck, leaving powder burns, but the bullet plowed harmlessly into the wall. As the two men locked in a deadly embrace, Blanck shoved the revolver into Cudihee's midsection, but the detective grasped the killer's gun hand, preventing him from cocking it. With his other hand Cudihee clutched at Blanck's throat. When both men fell on the bed the star was torn from the detective's vest, and Cudihee grunted, "You would murder me, would you?" and tightened his grip on the killer. Seconds seemed to pass into minutes as their deadly struggle continued, but the sound of the gunshot had brought Corbett running.

Crashing through the door, Corbett took in the scene. Reacting quickly, he struck Blanck over the head repeatedly with his revolver until the beaten killer cried out, "I give up, spare my life." Mad with anger, Corbett continued to strike out until Cudihee begged the policeman to stop.

"What did you want to kill Cudihee for? He never did you a wrong, he was only doing his duty," Corbett asked Blanck after taking his revolver. The conquered killer answered without remorse, "I might as well kill two as one."

Before Blanck could regain his composure, Cudihee acted on a hunch and quickly asked him, "Why did you murder that poor fellow last night?"

"Why didn't he give up the dough?" groused the bloody prisoner, still half-conscious. As an afterthought, he added, "I would have killed a hundred men rather than be captured."

As the two lawmen escorted their prisoner to the patrol box on the corner of Battery and Front Streets, Blanck regained his senses and vented his rage at Corbett for the beating. Seething with hatred, Blanck told the officer, "I would kill you for fifty cents. If I meet you in hell I will run a pitchfork through you." Taking the threat coolly, Corbett told Blanck that he should be thankful that he was not shot dead.

While waiting at the patrol box, word of the arrest quickly spread through the neighborhood and a crowd soon gathered. In no time the talk became ugly, and the throng began to shout, "Lynch him!" Blanck sneeringly remarked to the two detectives, "Yes, let them lynch me. I'd just as leave be lynched, but these stiffs won't do it."

When the patrol wagon arrived, Blanck was hustled aboard. As the wagon headed for police headquarters, the killer cooled down and callously asked where he shot the man in the Mug Saloon. When told the bullet struck the bartender in the heart, Blanck replied with another of his apathetic remarks, "He should not have made a break at me. Why didn't he give up the dough?"

That night the Seattle police searched Blanck's room at the Bay View house. They found the killer's cartridge belt with twenty .45-calibre shells in it.

The *Seattle Telegraph* satirically reported, "Now the happy murderer - Oh, he laughs when he tells of firing the bullet that pierced poor Charley Birdwell's heart - occupies the steel tank in the city jail."[3]

[1] *Seattle Post-Intelligencer*, October 2, 3, 4, 5, 6, 1894.

[2] *Seattle Post-Intelligencer*, October 4, 5, 18, 1894; *Seattle Telegraph*, October 5, 1894.

[3] *Seattle Post-Intelligencer*, October 5, 18, 1894; *Seattle Telegraph*, October 5, 1894. The victim's name was also reported as Bridwell, but Birdwell was the most common spelling.

PART II

IN A HURRY FOR THE GALLOWS

CHAPTER SEVEN

"Might Just as Well Die Today as Tomorrow"

Upon reaching police headquarters, Tom Blanck was taken to Chief Bolton Rogers' private office. When questioned about the saloon murder, Blanck again admitted to the killing and said that his name was an alias. Following the interrogation, Blanck was placed in the police station's steel cage. Rogers was so pleased by the capture and confession that he ordered a hot supper from the Tortoni Restaurant for Blanck, and later had a long talk with him. Taking his fate philosophically, Blanck asked Rogers if the state would allow him to choose hanging or shooting. "Well, the law here says hanging," answered the chief.

Suspecting that the prisoner was the killer of Puyallup Constable Jeffrey, Chief Rogers questioned Blanck several times about the murder. Each time the killer merely grinned, but finally said laughingly, "Well, I wonder if they ever got that man in the brush. I hope he got away." At this point, Blanck inadvertently admitted his presence in Montana at the time of the Flynn and Ogle murders. When Rogers had finished talking with Blanck, a reporter from the *Post-Intelligencer* received permission to interview the killer.

For the next three months Tom Blanck became a focal point for newspaper reporters. The remorseless, cold-blooded killer seemed to welcome the attention, although he answered many of the questions guardedly; however, these interviews offered an unusual glimpse into the psychological makeup of a nineteenth-century gunman and killer.

When the reporter entered, Jailer Henry Surry got Blanck off his bed. The newsman's first impression of Blanck was a pleasant, powerful, aggressive, but cruel young man with angry gray eyes set in a smiling face. The killer was dressed in a calico shirt and blue jeans. When asked if he was a burglar or highwayman, Blanck grinned and said, "On many things I would have to tell you lies, so I will not answer at all."

Advancing his age by weeks, Tom Blanck told the reporter he was twenty-four years old and a native of New York. Not wanting his family to learn of his criminal actions, he covered himself by claiming he was of German stock and that he was a bookkeeper. He said he tried to rob the saloon because he had only seventy-five cents at the time. He called Detective Cudihee brave but foolish. Blanck said his beating by Corbett was a "soaker," and the policeman's actions reminded him of perpetual motion-this phrase becoming a nickname for Corbett.

It was likely during this interview that Blanck adamantly denied he was of Irish stock, but said he had a Catholic upbringing. On the subject of religion, he stated that "in late years he had adopted a religion of his own, which in substance was that every person, after what was termed death, returned to the earth in some other form."

The questions and answers continued.

"Have you ever been in the penitentiary as a prisoner?"

"No."

"Have you ever done much shooting?"

"No, not very much," and then he grinned.

"Did you ever do any work in San Francisco?"

"No," was his answer, and then continued in good language, although with a foreign [New England Irish] accent, "I do not want to tell you any lies and many questions you would ask are such that I could not, for my own interest, answer truthfully."

When questioned about the robbery and killing of Birdwell, Blanck dispassionately replied: "I thought I was talking to sensible people, but as it turned out I was not. The big fellow [Codrick], instead of paying attention to my command, commenced putting his money in his pockets. Then I jumped on the bar and, when he turned, was undecided what to do. I jumped down from the bar and as I did so one of the men took several steps toward me and I, thinking he had a gun, determined to shoot before being shot. After I fired I knew he was hit, but did not wait to see how hard."

All sorts of schemes were tried by reporters and lawmen alike to pry information from Blanck regarding his background, and all failed. He told everyone he wanted to die on the gallows an unknown man, settling the matter with, "I don't want my mother to know the trouble I have gotten into."[1]

The newspapers also gave detailed descriptions of Tom Blanck. He was 5 feet 9 1/4 inches tall, light reddish brown hair, cold gray eyes, light complexioned, exceptionally well built with a small waist and wide shoulders and chest. His well-developed arms showed great strength. He weighed about 160 pounds, but looked as if he weighed 180. His face showed intelligence although his two upper front teeth were missing, undoubtedly the result of his frequent street brawls. There was no question that he was a very cool and calculating customer who grinned incessantly at his situation and fate.[2]

The next morning Chief Rogers had Blanck taken to his private room for a haircut, and then on to photographer Frank LaRoche. At first, Blanck's explosive temper erupted and he balked, but realizing there was nothing he could do he reluctantly cooperated. Rogers continued to question Blanck about the murder of Constable Jeffrey, but all he got was this sarcastic answer accompanied by a taunting smile: "I understand that the poor fellow they were chasing disappeared in the bushes and was then surrounded. If he hasn't escaped he must be nearly starved to death. I hope the poor man escaped."

Blanck also displayed his jeering humor by asking a *Post-Intelligencer* reporter, "The man who shot Jeffrey was seen by several parties and your paper printed a description. How do I compare to it?" When the reporter replied that the comparison was good and that he believed he was Jeffrey's killer, Blanck made this statement which was as close to an admission as he would give, "Well, I know a good deal about the matter, but don't intend to talk. If you can judge from my actions, all right." Blanck then grinned again, hung his head, and said in a low tone, "There are things I can't tell you."

Tom Blanck was then taken to Seattle Municipal Court for arraignment. Judge Joseph M. Glasgow appointed G. F. Bogue to represent Blanck, and the lawyer suggested that they fight the case and possibly get the punishment reduced to three years imprisonment. Blanck adamantly refused, stating he would rather be dead than serve three years. Chief Rogers testified to Blanck's confession, and Judge Glasgow committed Blanck to the King County jail without bond. Prosecutor E. G. McBride immediately filed the information and trial was ordered to begin within ten days.[3]

From the courtroom Blanck was taken to the county jail and turned over to Jailer W. T. Monroe who searched the prisoner and then locked him up in the desperate criminal section in the north corridor. A reporter immediately requested another interview with the prisoner, and Blanck responded readily.

"Have you any statement you wish to make for the public?" questioned the reporter.

"No," Blanck replied, "I don't know as there is anything special. I have thought the affair over and believe the jig is up. I might just as well die today as tomorrow. Even if I fight this case, I am sure to be convicted. The evidence against me is overwhelming. Struggle as I might, the conclusion would be the same. The best I could figure on would be a long term in the penitentiary. With me it is liberty or death. I had rather be killed than stay three years in the penitentiary.... It is all over and I am at the end of my rope, and the quicker the matter is settled the better. I can not stand to think of lying in jail two or three years."

With tongue in cheek, Blanck told the newsman that he did not rob banks because he did not have "two pals, horses, and Winchester rifles." He added that his intent was to travel along the Great Northern Railroad "collecting tolls," preferring to "get a few dollars and get away than to make a big haul and call the whole country after him."

The reporter then asked Blanck about belonging to a band of train robbers from Montana, which inadvertently enlisted this incriminating response confirming the killer's presence in Montana at the time of the Flynn and Ogle murders: "That isn't so. I am out here alone. I didn't think of bringing any men with me. I'd like to know how you found out I was in Missoula. I admit I was there, but only about three weeks. I came through Montana, but made no long stops nor did any work."

The interview continued: "Have you done any big money jobs?"

"No, I am a green hand at the work," and then he grinned in such a way that the reporter thought he was a liar.

"How much of an education have you had?"

"Only a common school training, and that in New York City."

Tom Blanck was covering his tracks and had told another reporter he was the son of an Illinois grocer. He ended the interview by stating he would plead guilty and let the sheriff hang him soon as he got ready. According to Blanck's alleged views, death was nothing, it was just like going to sleep.

That evening, King County Sheriff James H. Woolery, Detective E. A. Gardner, Pierce County Deputy Sheriff J. M. Hicks, Jailer E. Duval, reporter J. E. Ballaine of Tacoma and a young man from Montana visited Blanck in his cell. They all agreed he was not an escaped prisoner from McNeil's Island, but believed he was a member of John Brooks' smuggling gang and the murderer of Constable Jeffrey. The man from Montana verified Blanck's presence in that state.[4]

The consensus of all who saw Tom Blanck in jail was also recorded by the newspaper: "Every man in the jailer's office last night remarked that the man before him was the most perfect type of confirmed and desperate criminal he had ever seen. He denies that he has a record as a train robber and highwayman, but there is no question that is his business and that he is a 'high roller.' With him it is liberty and other men's money or death, no matter how soon."

The only mistake these men made was naming Blanck a train robber.

On October 6 at 9:00 a.m. Sheriff Woolery, keeping his hand on his gun, brought Tom Blanck into King County Superior Court for his preliminary hearing. The unemotional killer entered an anomalous plea of guilty to the murder of Birdwell before Judge T. J. Humes and trial was set for October 16.

During the afternoon, Blanck was again interviewed by a reporter and reiterated his death wish, stating it made no difference whether by a rope or a bullet, as long as it was quick. Feeling a bit smug with his recent notoriety, Blanck said to the reporter as the latter started to leave: "You can do me a favor. Please bring me the magazine *Review of Reviews*, and, if you care to, make the

63

announcement that anyone desiring to communicate with me may write in care of T. B., editorial rooms, *Post-Intelligencer*. I will consider it a favor. You might add that I shall not wait long for a communication."[5]

The last sentence was an attempt at black humor by Blanck to put up a show indifference to his upcoming fate.

[1] *Seattle Post-Intelligencer*, October 5, 6, 1894, March 23, 1895.

[2] *Seattle Post-Intelligencer*, October 5, 12, 1894, March 18, 19, 1895.

[3] *Seattle Post-Intelligencer*, October 6, 1894; Criminal Case No. 1069, State of Washington vs. Thomas Blanck, Murder in the First Degree.

[4] *Seattle Post-Intelligencer*, October 6, 9, 1894.

[5] *Seattle Post-Intelligencer*, October 6, 7, 1894; Criminal Case No. 1069, State of Washington vs. Thomas Blanck, Murder in the First Degree.

CHAPTER EIGHT

A Rose of a Different Color

October the sixth was a busy day; Mayor Phelps lauded the actions and bravery of Edward Cudihee while the newspaper reported that a reward was to be collected for the detective. The funeral of Charles H. Birdwell was held at 1:30 p.m. at Bonney and Stewart's Chapel, and his body was interred in the Lake View Cemetery. And that evening Tom Blanck's guilt as the murderer of Constable Jeffrey was established.

Frank McMurray was brought from Tacoma and hidden behind a screen. When Blanck was brought up from his cell, the young man identified him as the killer. Two Puyallup residents who witnessed the murder, hotel owner John Scott and Thomas Boulay, also identified Blanck as the killer. Blanck continued to deny that he had killed the constable.

Before his return to Tacoma, McMurray related the details of the killing and his association with Blanck in an interview with a *Post-Intelligencer* reporter. Blanck obviously had talked a lot about himself, for McMurray added, "He is pretty well educated, and understands phrenology from beginning to end. He is also an infidel who always said he did not think it made much difference whether a man was alive or dead." The boy also expressed his obvious admiration for his associates, especially Tom Blanck, "They were good to me, and I know would have fought for me. I am sorry for Hamilton, but don't see as it will do him any good now. He might as well be dead as alive."

Trying to elicit inciting news, the reporter asked McMurray if Blanck said anything about robbing trains. Not realizing the implications of the question, the boy replied, "No, but I guess he and his pals are up to that business together with 'strong arm' work. Hamilton had a fine, false long beard when I saw him last and was having another made in Tacoma. He also had a thing that went over his shoulders and came down his front to his waist. It was sort of a carpenter's apron, but train robbers use the same thing for passengers to drop their valuables into. I don't think any of my friends did any work in this section, but I know they were hard men...."

With a touch of vainglory for his erstwhile "partner," McMurray continued, "I did not know anything about the work Hamilton was doing here until yesterday, but I know that he is a desperate man and can hit the bull's eye every time. He always shoots for the heart and I guess prides himself on it." Little did the boy know how prophetic his final statement would prove, "I don't believe that he will hang. He had rather be shot down while attempting to escape."[1]

The next day a reporter confronted Blanck with McMurray's identifying statements. The prisoner just laughed, saying the boy must be mistaken. Blanck continued: "The boy evidently had an object in saying I was the man. If he matches that crime to me then his 'pal' will escape. If I did that murder I would have no object in denying it. It would make no difference to me." Blanck ended by saying he had nothing to do with the killing of Jeffrey, and would make that statement if standing on the gallows.[2]

On the eighth, Blanck had a surprise visitor, his Tacoma landlady, Mrs. Earle. In Jailer Monroe's office she came face to face with Blanck and, through fear, only identified him as the man who took a room in her house. When Blanck was taken back to his cell, she regained her courage and gave the killer a good tongue-lashing over the key business and his threat to throw her over the banister. Referring to Blanck as the "Jesse James of the Northwest," the *Post-Intelligencer* reported, "Thomas Blanck was unmoved, in fact he took the curtain lecture like a gentleman..."

At first Blanck said, "I don't think I ever met you," then added with derisive humor, "I don't think you are the woman I did business with. You are too large." The newspaper then commented on Blanck's insensibility, "Blanck took the matter lightly and laughed at Mrs. Earle just as he laughs at everybody who asks him if he killed Jeffrey."[3]

Blanck received another female visitor on the tenth. A unnamed Kirkland woman came to the jail after seeing Blanck's portrait in the newspaper. She said she thought he might be her deserted husband. Deputy Sheriff Jack McDonald, acting as jailer, took her to the Blanck's cell where he managed to whisper to the prisoner that the woman had come to claim him as her husband.

This infuriated Blanck, and his malice toward women was exhibited in his enraged response, "She is a God-damn liar!" The woman apprehensively faced him and immediately turned away, stating he was not her husband. Blanck hurled several coarse jests at her retreating back before the steel door shut off his voice.[4]

While reward donations for Edward Cudihee and John "Perpetual Motion" Corbett were building up in Comptroller Parry's office, Washington law officers futilely tried to establish the identity of Tom Blanck, whose clever alias summed up the result of their investigation. On October 11, Chief Rogers announced that he and his officers were convinced that Blanck was escaped murderer George F. Rose of the Red Rose gang.

The gang consisted of John Rose, his son George, John Edwards and a man named Gibbons. The first murder charged to the Rose gang was the 1884 murder of an old man named Pickler in Cowlitz Valley. In November, 1889, Jens Fredericksen and his wife took up land close to the Rose farm near Chehalis in Lewis County. Edwards ordered the Fredericksens to leave, claiming to own the land. When the couple refused, both were shot to death. The Rose gang was suspected, and, in January, 1890, a search was made for the bodies. When Fredericksen's body was found, nineteen-year-old George Rose confessed, implicating the others and leading to the discovery of Mrs. Fredericksen's grave.

George's father and Edwards were convicted and sentenced to hang, but the Supreme Court set aside the verdict and ordered a new trial. The two convicted men were moved to Oysterville because of lynch threats. At 1:00 a.m., April 11, 1891, a mob of forty masked men stormed the Oysterville jail and shot down John Rose and John Edwards in their cells. George Rose had been taken from jail at Montesano the previous November 30 by a band of masked men, and it was concluded that the men were aiding him in escaping; however, Rose was never seen again.

The descriptions and ages of George Rose and Tom Blanck were almost identical and both had the same manner of speech, fast but indistinct. On the eleventh, reporter Marcus Schelderup, who knew the Rose family, visited the jail. He said that the similarity was close, but could not swear that Blanck was Rose. Blanck adamantly denied that he was George Rose, but this did not satisfy Chief Rogers who telegraphed Pacific County for someone to identify Rose.

Meanwhile, Tom Blanck had tired of visitors and laid around all day in a hammock reading a novel titled *The Heiress*. On the eleventh, the *Post-Intelligencer* reporter brought the magazine Blanck requested. The smiling Blanck climbed out of the hammock and said he wanted it understood that he was not George Rose, and then lied, "I never did but one cruel act and that was when I killed Birdwell. I am willing to suffer for that."

The matter was finally settled on the fourteenth when Pacific County Sheriff Thomas Nolan came to the King County jail to identify Blanck. Looking at the prisoner, Nolan said the resemblance between Rose and Blanck was startling and then asked the prisoner to pull up his trousers. When Blanck refused, Jailer Monroe told him they would come in and pull them up by force. Blanck pulled up his pants and Nolan looked at the outside of the prisoner's right knee for a strawberry birthmark. George Rose was known to have such a mark, and when Nolan saw Blanck's leg, he stated emphatically that the prisoner was not George Rose. Tom Blanck went back to his daydreams and reading, waiting for the commencement of his trial.[5]

[1] *Seattle Post-Intelligencer*, October 7, 1894.

[2] *Seattle Post-Intelligencer*, October 8, 1894.

[3] *Seattle Post-Intelligencer*, October 9, 1894; *Seattle Telegraph*, October 9, 1894.

[4] *Seattle Post-Intelligencer*, October 11, 1894.

[5] *Seattle Post-Intelligencer*, October 9, 11, 12, 13, 15, 1894.

CHAPTER NINE

"Got It in the Neck"

One day before Tom Blanck's trial, his two court-appointed attorneys, John Fairfield and Daniel T. Cross, indicated to the *Post-Intelligencer* that they would enter a plea of insanity for their defendant and secure a commission to determine Blanck's moral responsibility. This was Washington State's first case in which a murderer pled guilty to a capital offense and was then put on trial to determine premeditation and sanity.[1]

Although Bailiff Brockaway came to the King County Court long before 8:00 a.m. on the sixteenth, a huge crowd was anxiously waiting to get a glimpse of killer Tom Blanck. The halls were filled with men and women, young and old, and when the courtroom doors opened there was a mad rush for seats. By the time court opened at nine, there was standing room only. The *Post-Intelligencer* had enticed the people with sensational reporting, calling Blanck both "the Jesse James of the Northwest" and "the man who handles a big Colt's revolver in regular Jesse James style," plus "the man who can hit a dime at thirty feet."[2]

A few minutes after 9:00 a.m., Prosecuting Attorney John F. Miller confidently entered the courtroom puffing on a cigar, soon followed by assistant prosecutor E. G. McBride. Defense counsel Fairfield appeared four minutes later. Within minutes the silence of the courtroom was broken by the rattling of chains, and every eye focused on the doorway. Deputy Jack McDonald entered, then came Tom Blanck, who was chained by his right wrist to Deputy George Cave, and following close behind was ex-detective John Roberts. Dressed in dark trousers, a dark plaid woolen shirt and a black slouch hat, Blanck sat down between Cave and Roberts and looked nonchalantly at the bench, paying no attention to the crowd.

When Judge T. J. Humes entered the courtroom, Bailiff Brockaway loudly called for order, and the judge called the case of the State vs. Thomas Blanck, Murder in the First Degree. Fairfield immediately took the floor and made a motion for a continuance on the grounds that he had not had time to prepare the case. When the motion was denied, Fairfield took an exception and made another motion, this time for a change of venue owing to the prejudice against Blanck in King County due to newspaper reporting. This was also denied, and the attorney took another exception. The rest of the morning was taken up with the selection of jurors. At one point, Fairfield asked a prospective juror, "If it should be shown that the defendant was not responsible for his actions, would you take that into consideration?" Blanck caught the question, bowed his head, but could not conceal the smile on his face.

Only seven jurors had been chosen by noon, and Blanck went below for lunch, eating a meal the newspaper reported "would have opened the eyes of a lion." At 1:30 p.m. court resumed, and by the end of the day a full jury had still not been selected. Blanck calmly sat through the ordeal with his chair tilted back and his hands locked around his knee, seemingly untroubled. Several times he nearly fell asleep. When Fairfield was asked about his client, he said with acquiescence, "Tom Blanck is a peculiar client and says very little. He is hard to talk with about his case, but apparently never worries." The attorney also said he would get no payment for his services.[3]

Tom Blanck slept like a baby, and the next morning ate a huge breakfast, enlisting this comment from Jailer Monroe, "Tom may be on trial for his life, but that does not give him dyspepsia or diminish his appetite." At 9:30 a.m., Blanck was escorted into the courtroom by Deputies Cave and Tom Roberts, and entered like a spectator, walking quickly to his seat. The morning crowd was not as large as the previous day, but by the afternoon it was back to full force. A large number of women were present and watched eagerly for the appearance of Tom Blanck. In the rush for seats, hats were knocked off and umbrellas crushed, but the women occupied the front seats. Bailiff Brockaway had to shout to maintain any kind of control. (Women usually did not attend these types of trials—and never got the best seats.)

The choosing of the jury was again deadlocked, and Sheriff Woolery had to bring in ten more prospective jurors at eleven o'clock. Within fifteen minutes the jury had been selected: F. G. Hart, 46, miner; Stephen Carkeek, 45, contractor; Amos C. Springer, 55, contractor; Frank Worth, 45, sea captain; Edward Seaberg, 26, newspaper man; Chilton Johnson, 46, farmer; M. Rounds, 61, machinist; M. McTeigh, 35, real estate dealer; S. J. Collins, 43, carpenter; John Lynch, 39, milliner; L. E. Palmer, 25, merchant. Amasa Miller, 55, a capitalist, was chosen foreman.

At 11:20, John Miller made the opening statements for the prosecution, speaking of Birdwell's murder and Blanck's plea of guilty. He reminded the jury it was their duty to simply determine the degree of the prisoner's guilt. Coroner Horton testified, followed by saloon owner William Codrick, who brought a smile to Blanck's face when he described the killer's exit from the saloon. At noon an adjournment for dinner was called, and Blanck was accompanied by Fairfield to the jail for a consultation.

Fairfield's cross-examination of Codrick resumed in the afternoon session.

"Does the defendant look now as he did that night?"

"His eyes look the same."

"How did they look?"

"Dead earnest," was the answer, and everyone in the courtroom, including Blanck, laughed.

"Did Blanck look wild or act strangely?"

"No, sir; he was cool and collected."

During the testimony of saloon patron Edward Spranger, everyone had a good laugh over his description of his clash with Blanck when he attempted to flee from the saloon. Detective Cudihee testified to his fight with Blanck and the killer's confession, and Chief Rogers told of the defendant's statement about the murder. Blanck got another good laugh when Amelia Hartley, who was nearsighted, had to approach him and peer closely at his face before commenting with a laugh, "I guess I know him." Miller then closed the prosecution's case.

Tom Blanck again sat through the proceedings with his hands clasped around his knee and an uninterested expression on his face. That evening a *Post-Intelligencer* reporter interviewed Blanck again, asking the prisoner how he viewed the court proceedings.

"I didn't think this business would last so long. I hoped it would be cut off short. Yes, the proceedings worry me so much that I can hardly keep awake."

"What do you think of the insanity plea?"

"Oh, it's as bad to be shut up in an insane asylum as in jail. If I had known this thing would drag along like this I would not have been here."

The reporter stated Blanck was a great eater and had enjoyed this aspect of being on trial.[4]

The third morning of the trial brought the largest crowd yet to see attorney Fairfield's line of defense for Tom Blanck. The number of women had increased, but so had the men, who were determined to obtain the best seats. All were in their chairs long before the trial was scheduled to commence at 9:30. When the clock passed the specified time, spectators kept their eyes on the doorway, but Blanck did not appear. If they had known what was occurring two floors below, they would have broken their necks to get down there.

At 9:25, Jailer Monroe brought Tom Blanck out of the steel tank and turned him over to Deputies Cave and Roberts. Cave took out his nippers, a short wrist chain with handles at the ends, one to fit through the other so painful, twisting leverage can be exerted upward. If Cave had seen the cold glint in Blanck's gray eyes, he might have been more careful. After Cave slipped the nippers over the Blanck's right wrist, the two deputies flanked the prisoner and started up the stairs. All went well until they reached the third step to the third floor.

With lightning speed, Blanck's left fist shot out and caught the unsuspecting Cave on the jaw. The deputy tumbled down the stairs, dragging Blanck with him. Roberts jumped down the stairs and caught Blanck by the coat collar, and a fight started in earnest. Blanck continued to strike out with his left fist, windmilling punches at the two deputies. Cave worked the nippers tighter and finally drew his gun from his pocket, bringing it down on Blanck's right temple with force. Blood spurted from the wound and cascaded down the prisoner's face. The fight finally went out of Blanck, and he cried out, "I will give up."

As the deputies took the bloody prisoner back to the jailer's office, Roberts said, "You are a nice one, Tom. What were you trying to do?" Blanck replied disgustedly, "Well, I'd like to know who the hell wouldn't try to escape under the circumstances."

Blanck was put up against the wall, and he leaned his head over and let the blood drip into a coalscuttle while Jailer Monroe went for dressings. Blanck, with an ugly look on his face, then sat on a chair in the middle of the room while Monroe washed and dressed his wound. The room was now filled with people, including "Perpetual Motion" Corbett, who said, "Hello, Tom, don't you know me?" In a voice laced with venom, Blanck growled, "Go to hell, you son of a bitch." "Don't talk that way," retorted Monroe, "the officer was only doing his duty." If the officers knew that the ever-dangerous Tom Blanck was just getting a second wind, they would have taken more precaution.

When Blanck's wound stopped bleeding, Cave told him to get up and come along to the courtroom. The defiant prisoner refused to budge. Both Cave and Roberts put their nippers on Blanck and told him to get up and walk. Blanck shot out of his chair and shoved his arms out with all his strength, trying to shake off the deputies. Again, the man went wild, his eyes glared as he hurled himself at Cave and then Roberts, his teeth gnashing as he tried to bite them.

Everybody reacted at once. Monroe jumped at Blanck's throat, but the speedy prisoner dodged the jailer and sank his teeth into the first finger of Monroe's right hand. Blanck held on like a bulldog until Sheriff Woolery clipped him with an uppercut to the jaw. Blanck twisted his head, removing a chunk of flesh from Monroe's finger, and continued to grapple with the two deputies. When Corbett and Monroe finally seized the maddened prisoner from behind, he gave up his struggle for freedom.

The fight was over, but Blanck's determination not to go to the courtroom was as strong as ever. Cave and Roberts took him by the arms while Monroe and Corbett pushed on his hips and shoulders, and the tenacious prisoner was hauled up the stairs. Blanck kept his legs stiff, getting leverage on every stair, and held back with all his might, kicking and bucking through the hallway to the judge's office. Some wag called it "making a feller walk the turkey."

While Blanck was in the judge's office, Sheriff Woolery went into court and called John Fairfield aside. The attorney was told of the on-going commotions, and the two men, with prosecutor Miller, walked to the judge's bench. The discussion was over consent to have Blanck chained while in the courtroom, and when they finished the sheriff left the courtroom. A few minutes later there was a noise in the hall, and the crowd murmured, "Blanck is coming."

Tom Blanck was literally surrounded—the sheriff in front, then came Deputies Cave and Roberts holding each of the prisoner's arms secured in nippers, and bringing up the rear was Deputy McDonald and John Roberts. When the berserk killer reached the courtroom door his demeanor took an abrupt change; he straightened up, walked rapidly through the courtroom, collapsed heavily into his chair, dropped his head to his chest and stared at the floor through half-lidded eyes. The red welt was evident on the side of Blanck's head, but none of the spectators knew what it meant.

This turn of events did not sit well at all with John Fairfield. He had subpoenaed several witnesses, newspapermen, county officials and experts on insanity, but when he was called to begin his defense he astonished everyone by simply saying, "I desire to say that the defense rests." Apparently Tom Blanck did not give his attorneys any cooperation, which left them no choice but to terminate their efforts to offer a defense.

Assistant Prosecutor McBride made the opening argument for the state. In a precise manner he confined himself to the facts of the case, pointing out that Blanck had plead guilty. John Fairfield then took the floor. If he held any malice toward Tom Blanck it did not show, and he gave an eloquent argument of defense. He reviewed the duties of the jury and stated that the reason Blanck plead guilty was as much a secret to him as it was to the jury. Fearing he was fighting a losing cause, the attorney spoke in his own defense: "I have no apologies to make; I have acted according to my conscience and the order of the constitution of this state. I have done my duty to the best of my ability to see that the defendant has lost none of his rights under the law."

Fairfield closed by admitting that Tom Blanck's actions were malicious, but not premeditated, and asked for a verdict of murder in the second degree. The *Post-Intelligencer* called it "one of the finest efforts ever witnessed in a criminal trial in King County."

Prosecutor Miller made the closing argument, figuratively roasting Tom Blanck. The more the lawyer vilified the killer, the more Blanck smiled. When Miller said in closing, "This most terrible of desperate criminals, who has shot down in cold blood an innocent person and tried to murder one of the best officers that ever

1069

State of Washington King County Superior Court We the Jury in the case Where the State of Washington is plaintiff and Thomas Blanck is defendant, do find the defendant guilty of Murder in the first degree and that the defendant suffer death

G. S. Miller

Foreman

Handwritten guilty verdict and sentence of death by the jury in the trial of Tom Blanck, October, 1894. Criminal Case No. 1069, State of Washington vs. Thomas Blanck, Murder in the First Degree. *Division of Archives and Records Management, Olympia, Washington.*

wore a star [Cudihee] should be wiped from the face of the earth," Blanck fought hard to keep from laughing.

In essence, the judge then sealed Blanck's fate: Judge Humes in his charge to the jury said that if a man pleaded guilty, under the law, it was the duty of the jury to find the degree of guilt and fix the penalty. He then defined the three grades of homicide in this state and said it was not necessary in the case at bar for the state to show that willful intent existed in the mind of the defendant for any length of time. And if the evidence showed that Birdwell was shot while Blanck was attempting robbery, it was not necessary for the jury to consider premeditation.

The jury retired at 11:40 a.m., with Blanck closely eyeing each one. They deliberated only thirty-five minutes, and came back with this verdict read by Court Clerk P. D. Hughes: "We, the jury in the case where the state of Washington is plaintiff and Thomas Blanck is defendant, do find the defendant guilty of murder in the first degree and that the defendant suffer death."

When the verdict was read, Blanck sat stoically with his eyes cast down, making no sign that the sentence of death affected him. The convicted killer was immediately hustled from the courtroom. On the way to the cellblock, Blanck asked Sheriff Woolery to put him in a cell by himself. The request was denied. Back behind bars, the convicted killer seemed relieved to be among the prisoners again, and when asked by his fellow inmates, "What did you get?" Tom Blanck jauntily replied, "Got it in the neck the first jump out of the box."[5]

[1] *Seattle Post-Intelligencer*, October 16, 1894.

[2] *Seattle Post-Intelligencer*, October 17, 1894.

[3] *Seattle Post-Intelligencer*, October 17, 1894; Criminal Case No. 1069, State of Washington vs. Thomas Blanck, Murder in the First Degree.

[4] *Seattle Post-Intelligencer*, October 18, 1894; Criminal Case No. 1069, State of Washington vs. Thomas Blanck, Murder in the First Degree.

[5] *Seattle Post-Intelligencer*, October 19, 1894; Criminal Case No. 1069, State of Washington vs. Thomas Blanck, Murder in the First Degree.

CHAPTER TEN

"That Court Makes Me Weary"

In the aftermath, during the afternoon and evening of the last day of the trial, clouds of apprehension and tension hung over the King County Courthouse and jail. What will Tom Blanck do next?

It was well agreed that Blanck was the most desperate criminal ever dealt with by the law officers in the Seattle area. Although Blanck had docilely allowed himself to be led back to jail, the sheriff and all the deputies, guards, and jailers were in a high state of nervousness and kept a wary eye on the dangerous and unpredictable prisoner. The only one who was calm and cool was Tom Blanck himself, for only he held the key to Pandora's box.

At the conclusion of the trial, John Fairfield went to the jail to see his client. Through the bars, the doomed killer expressed regret for having caused trouble and thanked the attorney for representing him. When Fairfield asked him what he wanted to do about fighting the case by appeal, Blanck answered offhandedly, "Oh, I don't know. Come around and see me in two or three days."

Later that day the perplexed attorney remarked to a reporter, "There is no use talking, my client is the most peculiar man I ever met. I could not get any information from him to use in the trial and am yet in the dark as to who he is and where he came from. I must say that I am interested in him and want to know more."

By now Tom Blanck was big news, and the newspaper reported another interview with the killer following the conclusion of his trial:

When a POST-INTELLIGENCER reporter talked with Blanck yesterday evening he had the same old grin and had lost his savage look. The man seems to have the faculty of appearing like anything from a good-natured dare-devil to a most brutal murderer. He was asked:

"What do you think of the verdict?"

"Oh, it's all right. I have not got any kick coming. I think it is just."

"Were you satisfied with your attorney?"

"Yes, he made a hard fight, but I knew he could not win it."

"Why did you try to escape?"

"Why wouldn't anyone try? That court makes me weary. I had rather be in the hands of a 'vigilante' than have to stay there and listen to the tiresome doings."

"What do you think about the insanity theory?"

"I don't want any insane asylum in mine, it's just as bad as being in prison."

"Now that you've got to die won't you tell something of your life?"

He thought a moment and then replied:

"No, I don't want to say anything. I tell you what to do. Come around thirty minutes before I am hanged and I will tell you a story."

"Is it a love story?"

"No. I have never been in love but once, and that was with a gun I had. I could not part with it."

The King County Courthouse around the turn of the century. Tom Blanck escaped from the jailer's office located in the basement at the back of the building. *Courtesy Museum of History and Industry, Seattle.*

Sheriff Woolery had Tom Blanck put into a cell with Henry Craemer, another condemned murderer. On the night of August 13, 1894, Craemer murdered Philipina Mueller and her baby Fritz in South Seattle, and was apprehended the next day. He was tried and convicted in September, sentenced to hang in October, and was waiting for his appeal to be heard in May. The reason Sheriff Woolery gave for not putting Blanck in a single cell was to prevent him from committing suicide. It proved to be a wise move by the sheriff, for Blanck had another plan in mind, and it did not include suicide.

A short time after Blanck was incarcerated with Craemer, he told the murderer that he was going to attempt an escape or give his life trying. Blanck's plan was to knock down the first man that entered the cell, either Jailer Monroe or the deputy on duty, take his

Artist's sketch of the King County Courthouse around the turn of the century. *Courtesy Division of Archives and Records Management, Olympia, Washington.*

revolver, kill him and then escape. Craemer refused to join the plot, and when his attorney, J. L. Green, came to the cellblock, Craemer told him of Blanck's plan. All the guards and deputies agreed that Blanck would have tried it, with or without Craemer, if the chance was offered.[1]

At lights out, a feeling of relief was felt throughout the sheriff's office and jail, and the night passed quietly. The following day, in a strange sort of fashion, Blanck offered what he no doubt considered a magnanimous gesture. Considering the strong passion he had for his guns, he dictated the following affidavit to Clerk of Court T. W. Gordon:

Clerk:

Please deliver to J. H. Woolery, Sheriff, my pistol, belt and cartridges.

Thomas Blanck

The document was witnessed by a fellow prisoner, Harvey Knowlton, and was given to Judge Humes, who wrote, "Let exhibit mentioned be delivered to Sheriff upon above order." So the man who was going to hang Tom Blanck was recipient of the most prized possessions of the condemned man.[2] The next day, however, the dark side of Tom Blanck would again appear. The dangerous killer's mood swings were as predictable as a shifting wind.

[1] *Seattle Post-Intelligencer,* October 19, 1894, March 24, 1895.

[2] Criminal Case No. 1069, State of Washington vs. Thomas Blanck, Murder in the First Degree.

CHAPTER ELEVEN

"I Want It Pretty Damn Quick"

Not once, before or during the trial, did Tom Blanck show any remorse for the killing of Charles Birdwell. In fact, he took no responsibility for his actions, laying the blame on the victim for causing his own death. And regardless of conclusive evidence, Blanck continued to deny that he shot and killed Constable Jeffrey. This was the state of mind of the uncompassionate killer when he walked into the King County Courtroom on the morning of October 20 to receive sentencing.

At 9:30 a.m., Tom Blanck was escorted into Judge Humes' court by Deputy Cave and Detective Roberts, his wrists secured in nippers, with Jailer Monroe at his back. When the judge asked Blanck if he had anything to say as to why sentencing should not be passed, the prisoner tilted back a chair with his foot and leaned over the back of it, put one manacled hand under his chin and stared at the judge with a cold, hard flash in his eyes. In a voice laced with venom, Blanck spat: "I will come back and haunt you. I won't have one gun then, but two, and when I tell you to put up your hands I'll plug you pretty quick." To emphasize his words, he shot both hands toward the judge as if he held two revolvers. He acted like a man gone mad.

Unaffected, Judge Humes pronounced the sentence of death and announced that on the day of execution a warrant would be issued. Blanck was still leaning over the chair, and in defiance he snarled, "I want it pretty damn quick." Blanck resumed his indifferent attitude, and the deputies returned him silently to his cell without incident. His wrath had been spent in the courtroom.[1]

On October 23, the *Post-Intelligencer* announced, "Thomas Blanck to Dance on Air on December 7." At 1:30 p.m., the day before, Judge Humes sent word to Sheriff Woolery to bring Blanck to the courtroom. Jailer Monroe entered the tank and told the pacing prisoner that he was wanted in the courtroom to set the day of execution. Blanck promptly answered, "All right." After putting on his coat and hat, he was handcuffed and escorted from the jail by Sheriff Woolery and Deputies McDonald, Tom McCory and W. B. Woolery.

A huge crowd was again in the hallways, and when Blanck entered the courtroom the mob battled to follow the condemned killer inside. For a few minutes pandemonium broke loose, but the officers soon restored order. Judge Humes completely ignored Tom Blanck and did not ask him to stand up when he announced that the execution was set for December 7, 1894, between the hours of 9:00 a.m. and 4:00 p.m. That was all there was to it, and Blanck was led back to the jail below. When Blanck was safely in the cellblock, Sheriff Woolery asked him how he felt about the proceedings. Giving the sheriff his familiar smile, Blanck answered flippantly, "Why, I feel relieved. I was afraid he was going to give me twenty years." Back in his cell, Blanck laughed and joked about his fate to the other prisoners, stating, "Well boys, it's fixed for December 7 next."

The judge later gave the sheriff the death warrant, and Blanck was placed in isolation in a steel cage in the women's section. A deathwatch was ordered, and officers were assigned to watch Blanck twenty-four hours a day. The cell was completely furnished so that Tom Blanck would not have to leave it until his death march to the scaffold. The *Seattle Post-Intelligencer* added that the wing where Blanck was housed "is commonly called the dangerous criminals corridor because it is made of the very best steel and offers a difficult field for saws."

The last and only legal execution in King County was that of John Thompson on September 28, 1877, when Washington was a territory. On October 23, the *Post-Intelligencer* reported, "As a result of this, the state has no scaffold of its own and Sheriff Woolery will have to erect one. This he proposes to do on the latest scientific principles, joining it together in a way that it can be taken apart for future use." The newspaper ended the article with this chilling point, "He has not yet decided whether he will adopt the drop system or the weight system, that jerks the criminal to kingdom come."[2]

On October 26, Blanck had a surprise visit, and one he did not particularly relish. William A. Pinkerton of the famed Pinkerton Detective Agency was in Seattle on business and went to visit Chief Bolton Rogers, whom he had met in Chicago. Pinkerton had nothing but praise for the police chief, and the two went to the county jail to view the noted killer. Pinkerton reviewed his visit for a *Post-Intelligencer* reporter:

> When Jailer Monroe admitted me to the jail the first man I met through the bars was Knowlton, the gold brick swindler. [Harvey W. Knowlton was serving a two-year sentence for swindling.] I know him as an old crook and he knows me well. We shook hands through the bars and conversed for a while. Knowlton mentioned my name aloud and that was a signal for a little excitement among the rest of the prisoners, so that when I got ready to go to Blanck's cell Blanck had hidden himself from my view and no coaxing on the part of the jailer could induce him to come out from the closet. Unfortunately for Blanck, while talking to Knowlton, I got a glimpse of him as he sneaked away into a dark corner, having readily recognized him from his photograph. I saw just enough of him to satisfy me he was not an Eastern man. [A criminal wanted in the Eastern United States.][3]

Another Seattle newspaper reported that Pinkerton made these comments about his visit, "When Blanck wouldn't come to the bars, I said, 'Well, he can go to some hotter place; I don't want to talk to him,' for I had already caught a glimpse of him, and that was enough to enable me to know that I didn't recognize him."[4]

On or about October 28, Tom Blanck's birthday, the killer and his attorney, John Fairfield, held a consultation regarding his appeal. When asked by a reporter if he was going to appeal, Blanck evasively said he did not know, that it depended on the decision of his attorney. Blanck then laughed off questions about William Pinkerton's visit, saying, "No. I never met him, and he does not know me. Why did I keep out of sight? Well, I didn't care about seeing him."[5]

The headlines and stories about Tom Blanck earned him a fan club of sorts, and he began receiving letters from people trying to reform him. He got a big kick out of an exhorting letter from a woman named Nellie Williams, written at the end of October. He also received a long-winded religious harangue from a man named Benson in Renton. Not wanting any more of the man's letters, he wrote this curt reply on Halloween: "Mr. Benson: Please don't waste any more time writing to me, as it will do neither you nor I any good."

The newspaper also reported that by November first: "His demeanor remains unchanged, and he is apparently as unmoved now as when first sentenced. His attorney has not been near him this week. No death watch will be put over him until it is definitely decided that no appeal will be taken of his case."[6]

Eighteen days later, however, things had changed, and when asked by a reporter, "Are you going to appeal?" Blanck responded, "I think so." The newspaper speculated on Blanck's actions, reporting that the killer did not think he could beat the case, but would have the possibility of escaping from the King County jail. The newspaper continued melodramatically: "There is no one who realizes more than Jailer Monroe the necessity of keeping a sharp watch on Tom Blanck, for Blanck would wade through blood to obtain his liberty. Once outside the jail and in possession of a gun there are few men in this county who would care to have anything to do with him." The article ended by praising Monroe, stating that during his stint as jailer for several years there had not been one jailbreak and that his watchful, piercing black eyes would daunt the killer, circumventing any of his escape plots.[7]

On November 20, the last day in which to file the appeal, Daniel Cross, one of Blanck's attorneys, served a notice on prosecutor Miller appealing the verdict and the death sentence on the grounds that the court overruled both of the defendant's motions. Under law, the defense had a five-day grace period to file the appeal in Superior Court after serving notice on the prosecuting attorney. In contrast with his charade, Blanck gave a deep sigh of relief. He now had a loophole to escape the hangman's rope by juggling the justice system.[8]

Days passed into weeks, and still there was no word regarding the appeal. The prosecution had filed a motion to dismiss the appeal on grounds that the time for perfecting the appeal had expired. And on the day Blanck was sentenced to hang, his attorneys were scheduled to argue against the prosecution's motion in the Supreme Court.

On December 6, the *Post-Intelligencer* reported that Blanck was uneasy and that he would not be surprised if he was executed. Despite his bravado, the newspaper continued, "he would rather not be the star performer in an act of that kind." Blanck nervously stated: "I don't know about this appeal business. [Sheriff] Jim Woolery might take it into his head to string me up without waiting to hear from the supreme court, and then I'd be in a hell of a fix." The scaffold that Blanck was beginning to fear was now constructed and stowed away. It was built so it could be assembled in fifteen minutes.[9]

As the minutes quickly passed into hours on the day of execution, Tom Blanck nervously waited in his cell. As four o' clock approached, a crowd thronged the jail corridors but the convicted killer kept out of sight by hiding in the shadows. When the hour of doom passed the crowd left the jail and Blanck breathed easier, resuming his indifferent attitude.

On December 10, Tom Blanck was granted a temporary reprieve by the Supreme Court to allow his attorneys to argue his appeal in court. The court denied the motion of the prosecution on grounds that even though the time for perfecting the appeal had expired and that the appellant had plead guilty, the court could not conclude that the appellant did not intend to avail himself of the privilege of the law, and therefore the court should not deprive him of that right.

Jailer Monroe brought the news to Tom Blanck on December 11, saying, "Well Tom, the Supreme Court has decided your motion." "Has it?" Blanck replied impassively as he turned away from Monroe. After several seconds, the jailer added, "The decision is that the prosecuting attorney cannot dismiss the appeal." Although the killer tried to hide his emotions, he brightened visibly.[10]

Apparently the *Post-Intelligencer* was annoyed at Blanck's

reactions and headlined an article, "A Coward At Heart." The newspaper wrote the following.

> Tom Blanck is acknowledged by all who have had dealings with him to be a desperate character when he has a gun in his hand, but despite his gasconade and bravado when the sentence of death was announced against him the impression is growing and becoming in the minds of many a fixed conviction that he is a coward at heart....

> A few weeks in jail have either undermined Blanck's bravado or revealed the fact that all his actions heretofore have been aimed at the public with a view of catching notoriety; at any rate a noticeable change has been seen in the prisoner. There is no doubt that he would be happy enough now to compromise with the law and accept a twenty-year term in the penitentiary instead of hanging by the neck - and he would not care particularly if there were considerable delay in the matter.[11]

Undoubtedly Tom Blanck had reconsidered his impulsive and defiant statement to Judge Humes about wanting the noose "pretty damn quick."

[1] *Seattle Post-Intelligencer*, October 21, 1894.

[2] *Seattle Post-Intelligencer*, October 23, 1894, March 18, 1895; Criminal Case No. 1069, State of Washington vs. Thomas Blanck, Murder in the First Degree.

[3] *Seattle Post-Intelligencer*, October 25, 1894.

[4] Unidentified Seattle newspaper article, dated October 25, 1894. C. B. Bagley Scrapbook, Vol. 4, p.51.

[5] *Seattle Post-Intelligencer*, October 29, 1894.

[6] *Seattle Post-Intelligencer*, November 1, 1894.

[7] *Seattle Post-Intelligencer*, November 19, 1894.

[8] *Seattle Post-Intelligencer*, November 21, 1894.

[9] *Seattle Post-Intelligencer*, December 7, 1894

[10] *Seattle Post-Intelligencer*, December 8, 11, 13, 1894.

[11] *Seattle Post-Intelligencer*, December 13, 1894.

CHAPTER TWELVE

A Master Stroke of Deception

For the next three months Tom Blanck languished idly in the King County jail, appearing to have no more on his mind than his appeal. However, beneath this façade, his mind was furiously concocting a methodical plan of action devised to achieve only one objective— his freedom.

Following his reprieve from the gallows, Blanck was placed back in the cell with murderer Henry Craemer, who was also sweating out an appeal from the hangman's rope. From December into March Tom Blanck was a model prisoner, causing no trouble for the jail staff. Although held in awe by his fellow prisoners, Blanck's sense of humor and easy manner overcame their apprehension. He became so well liked that they elected him judge of the kangaroo court (a mock court held by the prisoners).[1]

One of Blanck's cellmates, petty larcenist William Cosgrove, made this comment, which was printed in the *Post-Intelligencer*, about the killer, "He never took anyone into his confidence and nobody in ther [sic] jail knew anything about him." Cosgrove was wrong; Blanck formed a strong friendship with one prisoner, George Howe.

Howe was an electrician, not a hardened criminal, and was being held only on a minor charge. For some reason Blanck trusted the man and picked him as his sole confidant, telling only him his life story. When asked by a reporter, "Have you any idea why it was that Blanck chose you as his confidant?" Howe replied, "I really have no idea. He seemed to take to me from the beginning, and talked freely about himself, but of course he knew well that I would never say anything about him until he was hanged or killed while trying to escape." Howe also made the following astute remarks on Blanck's character and prowess with a gun, "That fellow had implicit confidence in himself to do almost anything when armed. He said that with a pistol in either hand he could roll a tin can up a hill."

Blanck obviously had big plans while in jail. The *Post-Intelligencer* apparently obtained this information from Howe:

> Blanck became somewhat confidential with one of his fellow prisoners, and said that he intended to hold up the bank at Snohomish if he ever got out of jail, and eventually work back to California, where, as he remarked, he had been successful in some small hold-ups.

> At that time he was thinking of escaping and what strange ideas popped into his head can be judged by the following: One day he was walking up and down the corridor, when he stopped suddenly and said, "I wonder how in hell a feller would go to work to hold up an ocean steamer?" Those who heard the remark laughed, and probably replied that the problem was too hard to be worked out, even on paper.[2]

Tom Blanck's friendship was offered to all but one prisoner—Harvey W. Knowlton, the gold brick swindler. Blanck despised him. Knowlton sold a fake gold brick to a banker in Aberdeen on November 27, 1893, and was captured the following January. In March he was tried and given a light sentence of two years because he informed on his fellow prisoners who were planning a jailbreak. This, plus feelings of rivalry, was the reason for Blanck's hatred.

During the election of Blanck as judge of the kangaroo court, Knowlton was his rival for that office. On the day of the vote, Knowlton spread it around that Blanck had never been in jail before, knew nothing of the rules of the court and, thus, was not qualified to be elected judge. When Blanck was informed of this jailhouse slander, he made a speech "declaring he had been in more jails than Knowlton ever saw, and knew more in a minute about the law of the court than his opponent did in a month." As a result, Blanck

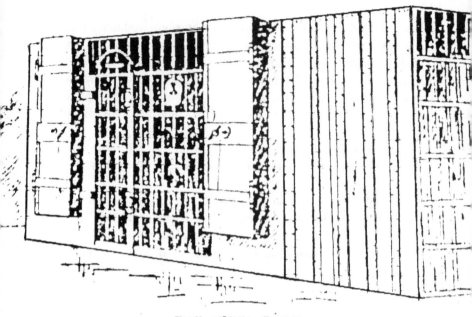

THE STEEL TANK.

Sketch made in 1894 of the steel tank section of the King County jail. From the *Seattle Post-Intelligencer*.

received just enough votes to win, twelve out of twenty-two votes. Following the election, Blanck was known to deal out "justice" in large doses, and Knowlton was the heaviest recipient of his inequity. In general, feelings of mistrust and disdain for Knowlton were universal among the other prisoners, but it was Blanck's overt rancor that terrified the informer; he was literally petrified of the killer.[3]

At one point during his incarceration, Blanck was visited by Peter Bruhn, the Fairhaven policeman he shot in 1891. Escorted to the jail cells by Jailer Monroe, Bruhn immediately recognized Blanck and said, "Hello, Slim Jim." Caught off-guard, Blanck replied, "Hello, Pete." Realizing he had given himself away, the killer tried to cover his error by quickly retorting, "Oh, I was mistaken. I don't know you." When Monroe walked away, Blanck dropped his pretense and made this snide remark, "Well, Pete, old man, how are you feeling?" Trying not to let his irritation show,

Bruhn answered, "I'm feeling pretty well, Slim Jim, with no thanks to you."[4]

In late January, one interesting bit of news was reported in Seattle's business newspaper, *The Argus*. This sardonic article was titled, "A Small Piece Of Business," and it likely gave Blanck a good laugh:

> The house of delegates is suffering from a relapse. The recent fit of generosity, in which they intended dividing the reward for the arrest of Blanck proved too much for them and they have now decided not to pay the reward. The next step will doubtless be to request the county to render young [Albert] Hartley a bill for Blanck's board during his incarceration.
>
> The reason, if it may be called such, that is given by the house for this extraordinary epidemic of frugality is that the officers, being in the employ of the city, were not entitled to the reward, and young Hartley did not make the arrest himself, nor was he positive that the man he had located was the murderer.
>
> It is well that the house of delegates has vouchsafed this explanation. Hereafter small boys locating desperate murderers will know how to proceed. Young Hartley should have entered Mr. Blanck's room fearlessly, with a United States cruiser in one hand and Fort Spokane in the other, and commanded, in tones of thunder, "Throw up your hands!"
>
> This order being obeyed, he should have proceeded: "I believe you to be a murderer—a bad man. You must be bad, because you smell bad. Will you kindly accompany me to a notary and make affidavit to the fact, and if you happen to have a witness or two in your vest pocket I would be pleased if you would trot 'em out. Then I will take you down, if you have no objections, and see if I can get the lawyers to permit you to be hanged."
>
> Hartley is young yet, and had he attended to all this faithfully there is hardly any doubt but what he would live long enough to get at least a portion of the reward.[5]

Somehow word leaked to Jailer Monroe about Blanck's criminal record in Montana, and Blanck unhesitatingly confessed to the Broadwater robbery in Helena, the barroom robbery and murder of Steve Grosso in Meaderville, the Marysville robbery and the murder of an unnamed Montana lawman, undoubtedly referring to policeman John Flynn. He said nothing about the other Montana crimes he committed. Blanck also told of the stage robbery in British Columbia, his early burglaries in Washington, admitted he shot Officer Bruhn and finally confessed to the killing of Constable Jeffrey. The newspaper stated, "In talking in a general way of his exploits he remarked that he had killed five men and probably wounded twenty in the past four years." You cannot hang a man but once, so Tom Blanck knew he had nothing to lose and confessed, but he remained adamant in his refusal to divulge his identity or anything about his early life.[6]

While Blanck was confessing his crimes, holding confidential discussions with George Howe and dropping humorous remarks, his mind was busy devising a plan of escape. This he confided to no one, with the possible exception of George Howe, whom he did tell that if he ever escaped, was cornered and had only two shots in his gun, he would shoot one of pursuers and then commit suicide.

Tom Blanck's plan was well thought out. First, he studied the habits of his cellmate, Craemer, who would generally read until midnight and then go to sleep. Blanck adjusted his habits and would sleep during the evening hours, rising when his cellmate fell asleep. When Craemer would arise in the mornings, he would find Blanck leaning over his bunk with his arms outstretched.

Blanck also observed the habits of his two jailers. The day jailer, Monroe, would never carry a gun into the cellblock whereas Jerry Yerbury, the night jailer, always entered armed. Yerbury would enter the cellblock exactly at 7:30 every evening for lockup and would not return again the entire night. In February, Blanck got a break when the King County Commissioners decided to do away with the assistant night jailer's position. Now the killer would have only one man to deal with.[7]

At the beginning, Blanck sat on his bunk after midnight for a few nights and made several rough drawings of Smith and Wesson revolvers. He then made a pasteboard model of the gun to scale. During the day he craftily collected bits and pieces of what he need-

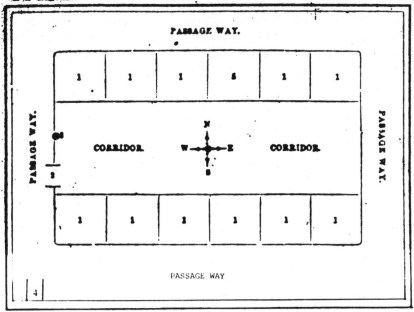

The cage is 22 feet wide by 42 feet long, and contains twelve cells arranged in two series of six on each side of a main corridor. The tank stands in the center of the room, with a three-foot passage way extending entirely around it. Following is a diagram:

1—Cells.   2—Doors into cage.
3—Little hole where holdup took place.   4—Entrance from jailer's office.
5—Where Jailer Yerbury and Knowlton were found.

Two diagrams of the interior of the steel tank portion of the King County jail, showing where the escape of Tom Blanck took place. From the *Seattle Post-Intelligencer*.

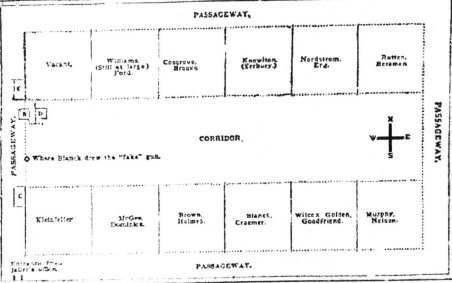

THE STEEL TANK AS IT WAS BEFORE JAIL DELIVERY.

C—Combination lock.   B—Outer door to cage.   D—Inner door.

ed until he had a stockpile of materials. When he had finished, he had managed to collect several pieces of wood; a small piece of basswood, part of a broom handle and a larger piece taken from a shelf made of spruce in his cell. He also gathered up four pieces of glass from broken medicine bottles, several strands of fine thread, tin foil from packs of tobacco, wire from the broom handle, which he heated over a gas jet near his cell, and a wooden awl. Blanck removed a steel shank from one of his shoes and finely honed it into a crude knife. In the early morning he would carefully hide his tools and materials in his bunk.

With methodical determination and precise craftsmanship, the normally impulsive Tom Blanck patiently made a graphically authentic reproduction of a revolver. From the larger piece of wood he carved the revolver frame, and from the basswood he made a two-part cylinder and the bullets. The gun's barrel was whittled from the broom handle and was rifled at the end. Blanck used the pieces of glass to scrape and polish the parts.

Blanck carved a fine line in both sections of the five-chambered cylinder and joined them together by pushing the thread into the slit and then tying it. He covered the incisions with chewing gum and soap. Blanck fitted the parts together and used the soap and chewing gum as glue. The trigger guard was attached by wooden pins, and the killer even took time to meticulously engrave screw heads in the appropriate locations.

When Blanck's creation was carved to his satisfaction he took a piece of charred wood and mixed it with food grease and soot from the bottom of a can the prisoners used to heat their tea. With this concoction he blackened the entire gun, covering any signs of wood fiber.

Blanck's masterstroke was the bullets, which he painstakingly carved to the exact size of .38-calibre slugs. For his plan to work the bullets had to look completely authentic, so he carefully covered them with the tin foil and worked them into the cylinder. The whole tedious chore took Blanck the better part of three months, and when he finished he had a masterpiece of workmanship. Professional woodworkers would later say that the cylinder and handles looked as though they had been turned on a lathe.[8]

All this Blanck was able to do under the noses of the jailers and the other prisoners without them having the slightest suspicion of what he was doing. Tom Blanck was now ready to carry out the second part of his plan.

[1] *Seattle Post-Intelligencer*, March 22, 23, 1895.

[2] *Seattle Post-Intelligencer*, March 19, 23, 29, 1895.

[3] *Seattle Post-Intelligencer*, March 21, 23, 24, 1895.

[4] *Seattle Post-Intelligencer*, March 22, 1895.

[5] *The Argus*, January 26, 1895.

[6] *Seattle Post-Intelligencer*, March 23, 1895.

[7] *Seattle Post-Intelligencer*, March 18, 22, 1895.

[8] *Seattle Post-Intelligencer*, March 19, 22, 24, 29, 1895.

PART III

GREATEST MANHUNT ON RECORD

CHAPTER THIRTEEN

"Thomas Blanck is Free"

In early March, the unconventional friendship between Tom Blanck and George Howe came to an end when Howe was released from jail. The *Post-Intelligencer* reported that Howe's unique relationship with the killer backlashed on him: "Howe said that after he was released from jail on March 11 he remained in the city a few days and then went to Victoria, where he had just commenced work when his name came out in connection with the Blanck case. 'It just killed me in the place,' said Howe, 'for when I walked along the street the people would point to me as being the man who knew Blanck. I got tired of it and left before I lost my position.'"[1]

Tom Blanck did not have to remain long in jail without a close friend, for six days following Howe's release he made his break for freedom. It was ironic that this New York-born Irishman would pick Saint Patrick's day to escape.

In 1895, March 17 fell on a Sunday, and that afternoon Blanck had a visitor. A woman known only as Mrs. Smith had taken an interest in the killer following his trial and conviction, and she appeared to be trying to reform him. Evidence found later would indicate differently. On Christmas she gave him a Bible, and on other occasions she brought him things to eat. On the Sunday in question she came only to visit him, bringing him a green ribbon for Saint Patrick's day. She later made this comment to a reporter, "When I gave him the ribbon, he took it, but said he would not wear it."[2]

For the rest of that afternoon and early evening, Tom Blanck acted normally, giving no indication of what he was about to do. Following dinner Blanck sat down to play cards with fellow prisoner William Cosgrove. Around 7:20 p.m., Blanck got up, went to his bunk and picked up the fake gun, carefully concealing it from the curious eyes of the other prisoners. He then nonchalantly walked down the corridor to the bars that surrounded the two cellblocks. Stopping before the small opening used to pass items to the prisoners, he took down a short piece of rope prisoners used to hang clothes on. Some of the inmates asked him what he was going to do with it, but he made no reply as he tied it into a running noose. Then he waited.

At precisely 7:30 Blanck's ears picked up the sound of the jailer's key turn in the jail door, and then Jerry Yerbury entered, armed and carrying a small bottle of medicine for one of the prisoners. When the jailer reached the small opening, Blanck whipped out the bogus revolver and said in a low, resolute voice, "Jerry, throw up your hands and don't move. If you disobey my order I will kill you. I do not want to kill you, Jerry, on account of your family, but it is a case of life or death to you or me." Yerbury lifted his hands.

Keeping the revolver in motion so no one would discover it was a fake, Blanck turned slightly as some of the surprised prisoners converged on him and called out menacingly, "Stand back all of you. If anyone moves I will kill him on sight."

Forcing Yerbury to come up to the bars, Blanck told him to turn around. Throwing the noose over the jailer's head, the killer commanded, "Here, slip that around your left arm."

"My God, what good will it do you, Tom, to kill me? If you do that you can't get out," the jailer pleaded.

"I don't want to kill you, but you must do as I tell you," responded Blanck as he slipped his arm through the bars and securely tied the rope around Yerbury's arm. The hapless jailer continued to remonstrate until Blanck bluntly warned him that if he did not do as he was told he would kill him and then commit suicide. Yerbury sensed the ruthless determination in the killer's voice and resignedly complied.

Blanck turned to convicted murderer W. A. Wilcox and ordered, "Here there, go and get me a looking glass." Wilcox brought it back in record time. Blanck then asked Yerbury if anyone was looking through the peep hole from the jailer's office. Receiving a negative reply, the killer pointed his counterfeit gun at the jailer's head and sent him to open the first of two jail doors. Watching Yerbury in the

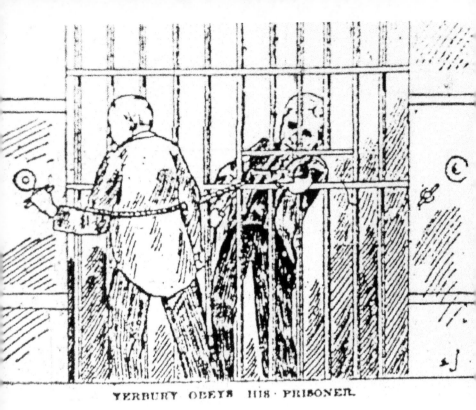

YERBURY OBEYS HIS PRISONER.

Artist's sketch of Tom Blanck's capture of Jailor Jerry Yerbury. From the *Seattle Post-Intelligencer*.

looking glass, the killer curtly gave the order, "Now open the next one." Tom Blanck now had the freedom to the entire jail.

Blanck quickly turned Yerbury around and took his .38-calibre Colt revolver, the jail keys and all his money—thirty cents. After lifting the jailer's watch the killer had a change of heart and returned it to his pocket, remarking, "Well, I don't want your watch anyway." Blanck then securely bound the jailer with the remainder of the rope. Adding insult to injury, Blanck removed Yerbury's gray fedora and jauntily placed it on his own head.

"Here there," Blanck fiercely called out to bunko (swindler) man Frank Hart, "go and get me Knowlton's coat." Hart fairly flew to obey the killer's command. After shoving Yerbury and the disdained Knowlton together in a cell, Blanck slammed the iron cell door shut and pulled the lever, locking them in. Tom Blanck was in complete control.[3]

THE CELEBRATED "FAKE" GUN.

Artist's sketch of the "fake revolver" Tom Blanck made and used to escape from the King County Jail. From the *Seattle Post-Intelligencer*.

Fellow prisoner William Cosgrove provided some comic relief, grammar and all, in his description of Blanck's break for freedom, which was cited in the *Seattle Post-Intelligencer*:

The whole thing was put through by Tom. That feller knows what he wants and the way he made the boys stand 'round when he was doing ther job was a caution. Old Knowlton was scared to death of him. I'm satisfied no one but himself knew anything about the play until he sprung it. He's a foxy guy, that feller, and tends to his own business. Why, I was playing cards with him only a few minutes before he made Jerry beg for his life and I had no idea that he was goin' ter do anything....He didn't like Knowlton because he was a trouble maker and a stool.

How he did make ther old man [Knowlton] get inter that cell! Then he would say to this feller: 'Do that' or 'do this' 'bring me that' or 'go get this' and you bet your life they got a move on. I

100

thought he had a gun, and I guess ther whole gang was in ther same fix....[4]

Tom Blanck's next act seemingly confirms the words of George Howe that when the killer got tired of something or had no more use for it he threw it away. Without hesitation, Blanck discarded the wooden revolver he had so lovingly designed and created. As he started to leave the cellblock, he dispassionately tossed it onto a shelf. On the other hand, this may not have been a case of indifference. As well as intelligent, Tom Blanck was clever and astute, and the act of throwing away the fake revolver could have been a "slap in the face" message to the authorities that all it took for the killer to break out of the jail that the newspapers said was virtually escape proof was the use of an imitation gun.

Using the jail keys, Blanck triumphantly unlocked the door to the jailer's office and slipped inside. Striding across the office, he stopped and paused before the last barrier between himself and freedom. Unlocking the door, the now-liberated killer euphorically called out to his fellow prisoners, "All of you who want to come, follow me."

Tom Blanck had shrewdly planned his break, but on his own he would be adrift. Now he needed help. Blanck turned to forty-five-year-old convicted murderer Servius Rutten, whom he knew to be an expert woodsman. When Blanck saw that Rutten was reluctant to make a break, he stared at him with his cold, gray eyes and said icily, "You are a damn fool, Rutten, if you don't go when you have the chance." Rutten went.

All in all, eight men fled into the darkness with Tom Blanck. The prisoners who escaped with Blanck, besides Rutten, were: William "Willie" Holmes (age unknown), convicted murderer; Charles Williams, age 32, charged with burglary; Frank Hart, age 30, serving seven years for grand larceny; R. H. "The Smoke House Kid" Ford, age 22, serving three years for burglary; Frank Clinefelter, age 25, charged with horse theft; C. W. Brown, age 28, charged with counterfeiting; William Cosgrove (age unknown), alias Slim Harrison, charged with petit larceny. Quite a nefarious group to be loose on the streets of Seattle, but none nearly as dangerous as Tom Blanck.

Eleven of the prisoners refused to escape, and two, James

Murphy and W. A. Wilcox, both convicted murderers, went for the police. Murphy got there first; rushing breathless into police headquarters on Yesler Avenue, he blurted to Sergeant Willard, "There has been a jailbreak at the county jail, and Thomas Blanck is free with a Colt's revolver!"[5]

[1] *Seattle Post-Intelligencer*, March 29, 1895.

[2] *Seattle Post-Intelligencer*, March 24, 1895.

[3] *Seattle Post-Intelligencer*, March 18, 1895.

[4] *Seattle Post-Intelligencer*, March 19, 1895.

[5] *Seattle Post-Intelligencer*, March 18, 19, 1895.

CHAPTER FOURTEEN

"I Will Have 10,000 Men Watching"

Seattle's *Post-Intelligencer* called it the "Greatest Man-Hunt On Record."[1] Newly elected Sheriff A. T. Van de Vanter vaunted, "I will have 10,000 men in this state watching for those escaped prisoners."[2] In the end, 111 men were paid by the King County Commissioners for serving as special officers in the hunt for Tom Blanck and his fellow escapees. It was quite a show—while it lasted.[3]

Tom Blanck saw the best escape route from the jail was the door in the jailer's office that faced east, leading to the back of the courthouse. Ironically, the killer had to cross the area where he was supposed to hang. Heading along the path at the rear of the courthouse, the nine fugitives reached Alder Street, where, after hurriedly whispered words, they split up in all directions. Tom Blanck would never see any of these men again.

Within minutes following James Murphy's babbled description of the escape, Sergeant Willard informed Detectives Phillips and Ed Cudihee. Rushing out of police headquarters, they ran into prisoner W. A. Wilcox on Seventh Street. "Hello there, Wilcox, where are you going?" asked Phillips. Crossing the road to the detectives, Wilcox answered, "I was just coming down to the station to let you know what happened." On the way out of the jail Wilcox picked up Blanck's fake revolver, and when he reached the two officers he remarked as he handed it to Cudihee, "The job was done with this, and I think you deserve it." With a laugh, the detective pocketed the prize.

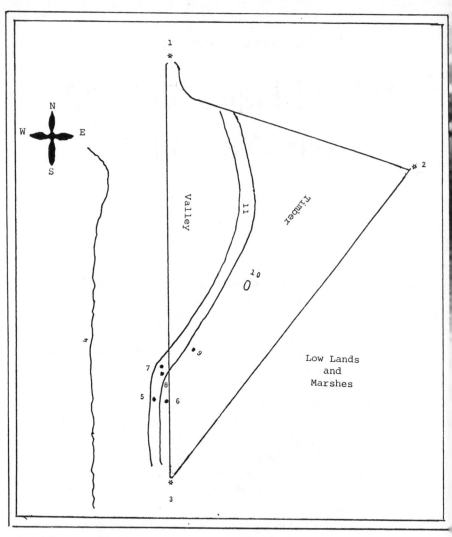

1-Black River Junction.
2-Renton.
3-Where the unused Northern Pacific belt line strikes the main road.
4-White River.
5-Kelley.
6-Burkman.
7-Where Blanck plunged into the brush to the west.
8-Rutten.
9-Tramp camp fire.
10-Jergeson's hill..
11-County road.
1-2-Columbia & Puget Sound railroad
1-3-Northern Pacific main line.
2-3-Unused belt line, with track..

Map of the Black River area where Tom Blanck eluded capture on the night of his escape. Redrawn by the author from the map in the *Seattle Post-Intelligencer*.

Cudihee later had some fun with the bogus gun, drawing it on some of the officers who thought they were looking at cold steel instead of wood. When the detective showed the fake to a reporter, he said in grudging praise, "There is no use talking, the man who made that knew what he was about. It is the best imitation I ever saw."

The three men hurried to the county jail where, with considerable trouble since Tom Blanck had the jail keys, they released Jerry Yerbury. Even when confronted with the evidence the chagrined jailer insisted that Blanck had a real revolver, stating later to a reporter, "Don't you suppose I know the difference between that 'fake' gun, as you call it, and the real gun Blanck had. It's no use talking, Blanck may have had that piece of wood, but he also had a real shooting iron."

While the officers were releasing the jailer, Sheriff Van de Vanter received the news and dashed to the courthouse. By 8:30 p.m., every town between Seattle and Tacoma had been alerted by telephone, and the list of escapees was wired across the state. Guard lines were set up from Tacoma east to Palmer and on to Franklin, Black Diamond, Renton and Lake Washington. The towns of Kent, Auburn, Orillia and Black River Junction followed suit.

Mayor Phelps quickly made his way to the courthouse and told the sheriff that the Seattle police force would be at his command to assist in the manhunt. Of course the *Post-Intelligencer* sent a reporter, and Van de Vanter made the statement about having 10,000 men watching for the escapees, adding, "I am satisfied that if we can keep the waterway points of exit covered we can run these men down in the woods tomorrow or within a few days."

News of the escape soon flowed over the city, and, strangely, a huge crowd converged on police headquarters instead of the courthouse, where the jail was housed. This fortunately left the sheriff and his officers unhampered, and Van de Vanter quickly issued the following rewards: $500 for Tom Blanck, $300 for Willie Holmes, $250 for Servius Rutten and $100 for the other escapees.

Seattle went into a frenzy. People milled around police headquarters and the courthouse with mixed feelings of apprehension and expectation. Rumors of holdups were rife across the city, and the police were deluged with inquiries. At 11:30 p.m. the fire bell sounded an alarm for a small fire on Eleventh and Jackson Streets.

The bell sounded three times three; coincidently, the old call for the vigilantes. Old timers of Seattle, reminded of by-gone days, armed themselves and rushed to police headquarters. Needless to say, Seattle residents slept little that night.[4]

All law enforcement agencies in Seattle and King County joined in the manhunt. Shortly following the escape, ex-Sheriff James H. Woolery arrived at the courthouse to help out and was immediately sent to set up guard units at the exits around Lake Washington. Seattle Detectives Philbrick and George Cave headed to Ballard and worked their way back to the city by way of Puget Sound hoping to cut off the fugitives. At Renton, Deputy Sheriff Tom Roberts rang the church bell at 1:00 a.m., waking the entire town. Within fifteen minutes half of the town's residents were armed and guarding every road. Ex-Detective John Roberts and W. L. Meredith were stationed at the point where the county road, the Renton Road, and the Northern Pacific tracks converged. Chief of Police Bolton Rogers sent his force to guard the waterfront from Ballard to Seattle, and Constable Fitzgerald, Tom Nash and a man named Groff spent the entire night guarding the Madison Street landing on Lake Washington. Ex-Constable Michael Kelley and Dick Burkman were sent south and unexpectedly met up with Rutten and Tom Blanck.

Burkman was armed with a double-barreled shotgun and Kelley was carrying a .32-calibre Marlin rifle as they headed south on foot along the county road. After crossing the Grant Street bridge, they were picked up by a carriage sent out by the sheriff and taken to Black River junction. When the two lawmen reached the point where the Northern Pacific Railroad tracks and the county road converged, they stopped and decided to set up an ambush. To the east was Jergeson's hill, where a small fire had been started by four tramps that were camped there. This was unfortunate for the two lawmen, for it was this campfire that aroused Tom Blanck's suspicions.

From the courthouse, Blanck and Rutten headed south on Seventh Street to Yesler Avenue and then headed across the Grant Street bridge. When they reached the brewery they ran into three men talking about procuring shotguns and hunting the escapees. The two fugitives quickly started talking about farming and leisurely walked by the men, who paid no attention to them. Continuing south, Blanck suggested that they steal some horses but Rutten disagreed, so the killer gave up that idea. The two escapees then concluded that they would either head for California or go east to the Rocky Mountains. In silence, they continued south on the same road Burkman and Kelley had followed. When they reached Jergeson's hill shortly after 12:00 a.m. they spotted the tramp's campfire, and Blanck became wary and alert.

The area around Jergeson's hill was very dark, and Burkman and Kelley only heard the sound of the escapee's footsteps. Burkman remarked to Kelley, "I guess we had better hold these fellows up and find out who they are." Kelley inched his way to the middle of the road and crouched down. When Blanck and Rutten were about twenty feet away, both officers cried out, "Throw up your hands!" Rutten obeyed and came forward, but Blanck raised his right hand slightly and began lagging behind. Kelley called out again, "Throw up your hands, there!"

"My hands are up," replied Rutten.

"No, they are not, and if you won't obey the command and keep coming I will put a hole through you," countered Kelley as Rutten crossed in front of him. At this point, Blanck dodged quickly to his right and plunged into the dense bushes.

Rutten walked straight toward Burkman, who demanded to know where he came from.

"I came from the county jail," replied Rutten.

"Who was the man with you?" questioned one of the officers.

"It was Tom Blanck."

"Hold this man," roared Burkman as he plunged into the bushes after Blanck. There were no sounds; there was nothing to indicate the location of the escapee. It was as though he had vanished into thin air, and it was likely that Burkman did not really want a confrontation with this proven dead-shot killer for he soon reappeared. The two officers stood for a while in the darkness and listened, but only the silence of the night was discerned.

Tom Blanck had escaped again; however, his worst fear was now reality, he was all alone in an area completely alien to him. He would have to make it on his own with the entire countryside dogging his heels, trying to hunt him down.

Rutten was hustled to Orillia where a telegram was sent to Sheriff Van de Vanter, informing him of Rutten's capture and the sighting of Blanck. The sheriff immediately set up plans to cut Blanck off between Orillia and Seattle. He made arrangements with Northern Pacific's General Agent I. A. Nadeau for a special train and handpicked the following men for the manhunt: Seattle Police Sergeant Willard, Detective Ed Cudihee, ex-Sheriff James H. Woolery, Captain Hogie, Deputy Sheriff Tom McCory, ex-policeman A. S. Stepler, Jim Bouchitt, Ed Winslow, Charles E. Love, ex-night jailer H. L. Smith, L. H. Brown, Niece O'Brian, H. L. Emery and Julius Redelsheimer.

The *Post-Intelligencer* gave the particulars of the operation:

Conductor H. C. Buckley and Engineer Duggar were routed out of bed and at 3:30 o'clock the throttle of the engine was thrown open and away sped the train. In order to make things more business like Deputy Sheriff McCory rode in the engine with a Winchester rifle. The members of the party were armed with rifles and 44-caliber Colt's revolvers. Cartridges for the rifles were not plentiful, but there were enough to have given the rifle holders a chance to do all the shooting they wanted if Blanck gave them a chance.

Kelley and Burkman, with their prisoner, Rutten, were waiting on the platform at Orillia when the train arrived. Deputy McCory disembarked and headed back along the tracks to Black River Junction while Rutten and his captors boarded the train, which left immediately for O'Brian Station. Rutten told the officers that Blanck had some railroad maps, but only one gun, the revolver he took from Yerbury. When the train reached Kent, Marshal Miller informed Van de Vanter that William Cosgrove had been captured at O'Brian Station by J. J. and George Crow and W. I. Stapleton, and was now in jail. Cosgrove was brought aboard the train.

On the return trip to Seattle, Stepler and Smith were left as guards at the spot where Blanck made his escape. At Black River Junction all the officers disembarked except Hogie and Redelsheimer, who took the prisoners back to Seattle. Winslow, who got off the train at the brewery, called in Deputy Jack McDonald, and the two headed back along the tracks to Black River Junction to intercept or cut Blanck off if he doubled back. At 5:30 a.m., the sheriff, O'Brian, Woolery, Brown, and Willard boarded a special Columbia and Puget Sound train, and Engineer Charles Houston and Conductor L. J. Lemere barreled the train to Franklin.

At Renton, the lawmen found the town up in arms over the escape. Willard left the train and worked his way back to Black River Junction while Woolery took the belt line across country to the main line of the Northern Pacific where he searched the area's barns and sheds without success. Constable Fitzgerald and Robert Lamoroux had gone to Sand Point on the trail of Willie Holmes while Cudihee went to Tacoma to see Sheriff Parker of Pierce County about guarding the rail lines to the east. When Deputy McCory reached Seattle, he had a humorous set-to with three local citizens who he thought were some of the escapees when he fired over their heads, scaring them half to death. The newspaper reported that there were 500 men on the trail of the fugitives.

At 4:00 p.m. on the eighteenth, a hunter named Hayes captured Frank Clinefelter near Kent, and he was brought back to the King County jail the next day. At Renton, Deputy Roberts boarded the train, and the sheriff's mind was eased when he found out that picket lines had been set up between Franklin and Palmer. In the forenoon of the eighteenth, Van de Vanter returned to Seattle for a few hours of rest before heading out again that night, while Woolery headed for Kent for an update on the manhunt. At noon he, too, returned to Seattle for some much-needed rest. The only lead was that Holmes and Williams had been spotted ten miles from Snohomish. Tom Blanck, the law officers' major target, was still on the loose.[5]

[1] *Seattle Post-Intelligencer*, March 22, 1895.

[2] *Seattle Post-Intelligencer*, March 18, 1895.

[3] *Journal Of Proceedings Of County Commissioners*, King County, Washington, Volume 9, pp.210-13.

[4] *Seattle Post-Intelligencer*, March 18, 1895.

[5] *Seattle Post-Intelligencer*, March 19, 20, 1895.

CHAPTER FIFTEEN

"I Will Never Sleep Until Blanck is Caught"

These words were spoken by Sheriff Van de Vanter on the night of the escape, and he relentlessly tried to fulfill them.[1] From that point until the night of the eighteenth, Van de Vanter was continually on the go with his ever-present deputy, Jack McDonald. From 9:30 p.m. until daylight on the nineteenth, the two lawmen covered twenty-six miles, and the sheriff still had the energy and fervor to encourage his men to stay on the alert. All told, Van de Vanter would go sixty-two straight hours without sleep.

On the morning of the nineteenth ex-Detective John Roberts brought word to the sheriff that Blanck had been sighted and positively identified a few miles north of Renton. Roberts and Meredith had followed Blanck's path for forty rods but then lost the trail. Ex-Sheriff Woolery and Deputy McDonald were immediately sent to the area, but they also lost the fugitive's track in the dense woods. The sheriff expressed his opinion "that Blanck was hemmed in and could not possibly get away."

At 11:00 p.m., the sheriff and McDonald finally went to bed at Renton, only to be awakened moments later by gunshots at Black River. The sheriff reluctantly climbed out of bed, walked to Black River and searched the area in pouring rain. At 5:30 the next morning the sheriff mounted his horse and raised a posse at Kent and headed for Black River.

On the twentieth, the *Post-Intelligencer* reported:

The majority of the deputies who went out last Monday [March

18] are still in the field and more men are going out constantly. Sheriff Parker, of Pierce County, is at Weston with part of his posse, guarding the approach to the Stampede tunnel on the Northern Pacific main line. The list of men as near as can be obtained is as follows: C. J. Garvey, J. B. McArthur, J. D. Woodward, C. A. Jones, W. H. Ducommer, J. T. Hillman, R. M. Shannon, J. H. Harris, M. Garrett, A. M. Cheasney, J. M. Cotner and Jack Keating.

On the twenty-second, the newspaper gave this list of men who formed the sheriff's posse:

Regular deputies - Jack McDonald, Thomas McCory, Thomas Roberts.

Volunteer deputies - Ex-Sheriff James H. Woolery, Chief Bolton Rogers, Mike Kelley, B. J. Keith, John Roberts, Capt. Hogie, Gil Philbrick, Detective Hart, Ed Cudihee, Capt. [sic: Sergeant] F. Willard, James Wells, John Huff, John Stevens, Nick Hanna, Terry King, Constable Fitzgerald, Charles Springer, Jake Julian, Ren Julian, Ed Moore, Ed Shea.

Volunteer deputies of Auburn - William McMahon, Pat McMahon, Dan Woolery, Mr. Bissel, Walter Lumm, Harry Pauley.

Rumors and false information continued to filter into Seattle. Ford was reportedly captured at Meeker and jailed at Puyallup. A suspicious man who eluded guards at Sumner was headed for Puyallup, and Williams and Holmes were still presumed to be in the vicinity of Snohomish. Holmes was also supposedly sighted boarding a train at Black River and dropped off near Seattle, so Sergeant Willard was sent out to investigate the matter. Five or six shots were reportedly fired near Black River Junction at 11:00 p.m. on the nineteenth, but no one could substantiate the claim. Chief of Police Rogers stated that Snohomish was well guarded, and that he knew nothing of any arrests. The only certainties were that, on the nineteenth, the King County Board of Commissioners authorized the rewards offered for the escapees, and night jailer Jerry Yerbury was discharged and replaced by H. G. Thornton.[2]

The *Post-Intelligencer*, diligently keeping track of the manhunt, reported:

> The scene of action in the hunt for Thomas Blanck was changed yesterday [March 20] from the dense woods between the Northern Pacific railroad and Renton to the thickly wooded country between the latter place and Kent. This action signifies that those that are conducting the chase believe that Blanck got through the lines around Renton and made his way south instead of doubling back north along the unused Belt line track.
>
> All sorts of stories can be heard concerning Blanck, and the proverbial report that he was "surrounded" made its appearance yesterday. Up to evening, however, not one of the deputies who returned from the scene of action knew anything about a hot chase after him.

Detectives Cudihee, Phillips, Philbrick and Captain Hogie caught the first train out of Seattle to Black River Junction on the morning of the twentieth. Here they met Sheriff Van de Vanter and sixty deputies. Chief Rogers also drove out to the area for a conference with the sheriff and returned to the city with Cudihee. The sheriff's force then headed to the place where Blanck was last seen near Renton, spread out and plowed their way through the dense woods. The search was fruitless, and, after having lunch at Renton, the posse swept the countryside toward Kent.

Seattle resident Frank Twiebell tried, but failed, to obtain a bloodhound to trail Blanck. Ex-Sheriff Woolery stated that the bloodhounds did not have enough training to be of service, so that idea was abandoned.

Again rumors flew thick and heavy. Special Deputy F. A. Iverson, who had been sent out toward Renton by way of Rainier Avenue the night of the escape, reported that when he headed home at dusk on the nineteenth, he saw a man he thought was Blanck passing through the bushes near the electric line terminus. Upon searching the area all he found was a black hat band. Another tale was that Blanck had returned to the same place he had been seen in

An older map of Seattle and surrounding area, showing a view more relative to the time period of Tom Blanck's escapades.

Artist's sketches of Sheriff A. T. Van de Vanter (left) and jailer W. T. Monroe (right). From the *Seattle Post-Intelligencer*.

JAILER W. T. MONROE.

Renton, but investigating deputies found it was just another false lead.

Special Deputies Stepler and Smith, who had been on guard duty near Black River Junction since the night of the escape, returned to Seattle on the late train Wednesday night. Smith stated that there were no shots fired in the area on Tuesday night, as had been reported, and that "Blanck had not been seen or heard of."

A more reliable lead came from Auburn, a few miles south of Kent. Early in the morning of March 20, Blanck was sighted at a farmhouse three-quarters of a mile from the town. The fugitive headed west into the Stuck Flats. The guards at Auburn were notified, as were those stationed at Puyallup and Sumner. Soon the flats were swarming with members of Sheriff Parker's posse and were later reinforced by King County deputies from Kent.[3]

At 4:30 that afternoon, Sheriff Van de Vanter and Deputy Sheriff McDonald headed for Auburn on horseback in a hailstorm. They made the ten-mile trip in forty minutes and joined in the hunt. On foot they plunged through sixteen miles of swampy terrain that the newspaper claimed "would deter ninety-nine men out of every 100." At 10:30 that night Van de Vanter got called to Sumner, where he again spent a sleepless night. The next morning, after traveling fifty-five miles in wet clothes, on horseback, in twenty-four hours, the sheriff arrived at Kent and cautioned his men to be ready to move in case of any new developments. The exhausted sheriff still had enough energy and equanimity to make this statement of appreciation to a *Post-Intelligencer* reporter: "I am under particular obligations to Chief of Police Rogers, Sheriff Parker of Pierce County, Sheriff Hagen of Snohomish, and ex-Sheriff Woolery for their assistance in covering the country to prevent Blanck's escape. Sheriff Parker has had sixteen men continually in the field from Sunday night. I shall push the chase after the rest of the fugitives, and expect to capture them in a few days."

The hunt continued throughout the day, and many thought Blanck had broken through the lines and was headed for Auburn again. By Wednesday night the exhausted deputies could do no more than rest on their arms and wait. The result was the same, Tom Blanck had vanished again.[4]

Unknown to the hunter and the hunted, the chase was almost over. The sheriff would not spend another sleepless night. And Tom Blanck was unaware that he faced another danger besides the relentless pursuit of the mass of men hunting him; he was slowly dying on his feet.

---

[1] *Seattle Post-Intelligencer*, March 18, 1895.

[2] *Seattle Post-Intelligencer*, March 20, 21, 22, 1895; *Journal Of Proceedings Of County Commissioners, King County, Washington, Volume 9*, p.110.

[3] *Seattle Post-Intelligencer*, March 21, 1895.

[4] *Seattle Post-Intelligencer*, March 22, 1895.

CHAPTER SIXTEEN

"Everything is Pleasant and Lovely"

Following his plunge into the thick brush near Black River Junction, Tom Blanck, cool, composed and deliberate, undoubtedly waited for the lawmen to show their faces. Blanck was fresh and would not have been afraid of any confrontation. But no one appeared, and when Kelley and Burkman took Rutten to Orillia, the crafty killer cautiously followed them and took a circular route around the train station.[1]

Blanck headed east, and two and a half miles above Renton he found refuge in a hay mow belonging to A. R. Peterson. Fairly comfortable and with time on his hands, Blanck displayed his mocking humor by carving the following in the handle of Yerbury's revolver, "T. B. from Yerbury, March 17."

Blanck apparently found some horse blankets and, whether for warmth or fear of being shot in the back, he sewed twenty-one thicknesses of the blankets into the back of Knowlton's coat. George Howe later made these comments to a reporter: "Do you remember how much talk there was about those patented bullet-proof cloth coats? Well, Tom heard of them and said he wished he had one. I have an idea he got the idea of putting the padding in his coat from that."

In the early morning hours of the eighteenth, Tom Blanck wrote a letter to his old friend Howe, which was found by lawmen on March 23 in the farmer's hay mow. Beside the letter, the officers also found the little piece of green St. Patrick's day ribbon given to

Blanck by the mysterious Mrs. Smith. Although Blanck's grammar is faulty, the content is notably thought-provoking:

Monday dont know what time

March 18, 1895

Friend Howe, it may have kind of puselt [puzzled] you why I made that break in shuch [such] a hury [hurry]. now I do explain it to you and you will think different. you know the girl wich [which] came up to see me. she write a letter to you wich you got from the post Office. at least I think you did because she told me so. well I think you gave her a letter to give to me Sunday 17 when she came up but she told me this friend of mine did not see her at all. then I kind of tumellet [tumbled] that she cept [kept] the letter or give it to Monroe I dont think you would not do what you toled [told] me you was going to do, so after I listened to what the girl had to say I thought that me and you could not comincate [communicate] anyway providing that was the case. but then for all I know you may not have seen her as what she said anyway you can let me know in your letter to me.

so after you got turned up [discharged from jail] I whittled out that gun wich I held Jerry up with in case it would come to a close call. if they had searched the cells they would have taken it away and then I could not have known what you intended to do then I would have ben [been] in a hel [hell] of a fix. the reason I did not lock the dorr [door] was if there were any personers [prisoners] that did not make up their minds quick enough to go they could go afterwards.

I and Lansman [Rutten] were together for a while but when we came up to a crose [cross] road there were some men behind a stump toled us to trow [throw] up our hands. Lons stood there. he would not run away. it would have been no good for me to shoot at them behind a stump so I ran away. Lons could have don [done] the same if he wanted to.

I am in the woods right hand side of cent [Kent] toward Seatle

[Seattle]. everything is pleasant and lovely. will meet you in 'Frisco let me know what place in your letter. sent [send] my letter to Portland, Or.

My name

JAMES MENDELL

yours truly TOM BLANCK

The woman referred to in the letter was the Mrs. Smith who was supposedly trying to reform the killer. Blanck alertly saw his opportunity when she first visited him and turned off his animosity toward women, turned on the charm and doubtlessly conned her into acting as his contact with the outside world. She adamantly denied this. There also was a mix-up between the identities of George Howe's wife Minnie and this woman. When interviewed later by a *Post-Intelligencer* reporter, Mrs. Smith remarked: "There seems to be an impression that I and 'Minnie' are one in the same person. This is not so because I never met Howe or have any idea who 'Minnie' is. I took a kindly interest in Blanck, but never talked with him about any attempt to escape or had any idea of what he intended to do. It was unfortunate that I called on him as I did."

The reporter bored in, "Will you state positively that you took no part in procuring the 'fake' gun for Blanck or smuggled it into the jail for him?"

The woman replied indignantly, "I certainly did not have anything to do with the gun, and know absolutely nothing about how he got it, except what I have read."

Mrs. Smith likely had nothing to do with the bogus gun or the escape, but she undoubtedly was Blanck's contact with his friends and was ashamed and afraid to admit it. The letter was not written as a condemnation of the woman, or to cause trouble for her, it was an expression of Blanck's bewilderment and frustration over Howe's actions.

Howe likely knew more about Blanck's escape plans than he admitted. When a reporter asked him about Blanck's fake revolver, Howe defensively replied, "Well, I don't want to talk about that now," indicating that he may well have furnished Blanck with the

119

materials to construct it, as Blanck was under more scrutiny than Howe. His friendship with the killer was obviously double-sided; Howe could hide under the wing of the jail's top dog if he became the top dog's gofer.

It may have been idle jail talk to Howe, but the two apparently made plans to meet later in San Francisco. The last sentence in the letter indicates that Blanck intended to head for Portland, Oregon, and wanted Howe to contact him there under his new alias, James Mendell.[2] Further indication that Howe and Blanck had made some sort of plans or understanding is evidenced in Howe's response to this letter purported to be written by him to Jailer W. T. Monroe the day following Blanck's escape:

Seattle, March 18, 1895

Friend Monroe,

When Van [Sheriff Van de Vanter] gives up hope of Tom, if he will pay my expenses I will get his man. I leave for Victoria tonight, but any time you want me Minnie will write or telegraph.

GEORGE

When a *Post-Intelligencer* reporter confronted Howe with the letter, he gave this rebuttal: "I have no explanation to offer at present about the letter published in the *Press-Times* [and the *Post-Intelligencer*] as coming from me and agreeing to tell where Blanck was if the sheriff could not find him. All I will say is that I would not have given him up for $5,000, yes, $10,000. In fact, I would not have thought of such a thing as surrendering him under any conditions."[3]

Why Blanck left the letter in the hay mow is unknown, but it is probable that he saw Peterson come out for early morning chores and forgot it in his haste to avoid detection. By 9:00 a.m., Blanck had arrived at the door of a schoolhouse a short distance north of Renton. He asked the schoolteacher, Ella Nitcher, if he could get some food. When she informed him that he was at a schoolhouse, Blanck replied, "Oh, I see." Turning, the killer pointed to a house some distance away and asked, "Who lives there?"

120

"Mr. Bassett," she answered.

"Is he an officer?" queried Blanck.

Becoming curious at this line of questioning, the teacher answered, "He is a school officer."

Blanck then threw out another odd question, "Does he take the morning newspaper?"

Upon being told that she did not believe Bassett did, Blanck started to counter with a cover-up reply, "Well, I'm looking for a job, and..."

At this point the schoolteacher interrupted him, commenting as she pointed to Bassett, "There he is now, you can see him yourself."

Referring to Blanck as the "monster of the Pacific northwest," the *Post-Intelligencer* reported the following:

> Miss Nitcher said that her visitor smiled when talking, and spoke so low that it was difficult to hear what he said. He was perfectly calm and cool and was rather pleasant to talk with. She took special notice of his hands, which showed by appearance that he had not done any work for a long time. When he talked he kept his head down and his hat pulled down slightly on his forehead.

> The man thanked her and went direct to Mr. Bassett and asked for work or food. The good farmer said he had no work to offer, but he would give him some food. Then he brought out a half a loaf of bread and a large chunk of butter.

> The man took the eatables and offered in payment 30 cents, a remarkable coincidence considering that Blanck took 30 cents from Night Jailer Yerbury. Mr. Bassett refused to take the money and his visitor, after informing him that he had two companions on the hill after wood, walked away.

From Bassett's house, Blanck headed east up a small hill into the woods. Special Deputies Roberts and Meredith had been on guard all night a short distance from the schoolhouse, and at 11:00 a.m. they started down the Renton road, stopped at the schoolhouse and discovered that Blanck was in the area. From Bassett's they followed the killer's tracks into the woods where they lost the trail.

Blanck lay in hiding until midafternoon and then came down the

Renton road and bummed some food from schoolchildren. It was now raining, and Blanck headed south on the Renton road until he found refuge in a barn belonging to Dr. H. B. Bagley. Early in the evening, Dr. Bagley went to the barn to escape the rain and spotted Blanck hiding under a shed. The doctor said nothing and went into his house.

Later that evening, Bagley went back to his barn and found Blanck still there. When the doctor told him to leave because he thought he was one of the escapees, Blanck just laughed. The killer arose from his hiding place, leisurely walked a short distance and then jumped the fence only to run face to face into several deputies. When ordered to stop, Blanck took off running and several ineffectual shots were fired at him.[4]

For Tom Blanck, things would continue to go downhill, and fast. Forced to leave the comfort of Bagley's barn, Blanck trudged westward through the woods in the raw, wet Pacific Coast weather. Within minutes the fugitive was soaked to the skin, and from that point on he never got dry. His clothing consisted of a pair of cheap, dark trousers, a black alpaca shirt, Knowlton's gray overcoat and an old, checked silk handkerchief tied around his neck. Blanck wore the same pair of shoes he wore when he was arrested the previous fall, and, in place of socks, he had cotton bandanna handkerchiefs wrapped around his feet.

As the manhunt intensified, Blanck was compelled to hide out in the dense woods between the Northern Pacific Railroad tracks and Renton, unless he was fortunate enough to find some kind of temporary shelter. By the evening of the nineteenth, Blanck had had enough, and the cagey escapee broke through the ranks of lawmen near Renton and laboriously traveled twelve miles south to Auburn by following the Northern Pacific tracks.

At 5:00 a.m. on the twentieth, having gone for thirty-six hours or more in the wet cold without food and sleep, the desperate killer stopped at a farmhouse three-quarters of a mile southwest of Auburn and was given a glass of milk. Knowing the relentless manhunters would soon pick up his track, Blanck left the house and headed westward into the inhospitable swampy terrain of Stuck Flats. By that afternoon not only did Blanck have the lawmen on his trail again, but also he had to find his way out of the swamp in a driving, bone-chilling hailstorm. Driven like prey before a predator, Blanck was forced to spend another miserable, rain-drenched night without sleep, food and shelter.

The weather finally took its toll; because of his weak lungs, he was now suffering from the first stages of pneumonia, which was confirmed by a postmortem examination. By the twenty-first, Blanck was experiencing acute attacks of shivering, shortness of breath and cyanosis, a condition where the body turns blue because of insufficient aeration of the blood. His motor skills were almost gone, and at times he was delirious and imbalanced. His mental powers also deteriorated, his judgment was poor, and there were intervals where he walked around in a stupor. Tom Blanck was finally confronted with a situation he could not control, and it brought him down.[5]

[1] *Seattle Post-Intelligencer*, March 19, 1895.

[2] *Seattle Post-Intelligencer*, March 23, 1895.

[3] *Seattle Post-Intelligencer*, March 23, 29, 1895.

[4] *Seattle Post-Intelligencer*, March 20, 21, 1895.

[5] *Seattle Post-Intelligencer*, March 21, 22, 1895; Interview with Dr. Josephine Newell, M. D., Raleigh, North Carolina, June 22, 1992.

PART IV

BLANCK IS NO MORE

CHAPTER SEVENTEEN

"Brought to Earth by Cold Lead"

Late in the afternoon of the twenty-first, Tom Blanck surfaced at the farmhouse of James S. Nelson, a mile east of Orillia. As Nelson told the story:

Shortly before 4 o'clock Thursday afternoon, as I was doing some work in the rear of my house, my hired man came up to me and told me excitedly that Blanck was at the front door a few moments before and he thought was now in the house. At this startling information I immediately went through the kitchen door and there, seated at the table, was none other than the notorious desperado, Tom Blanck, whom I recognized at once from a picture shown to me a day or two before by Sheriff Van de Vanter. My wife was setting him out something to eat, and as I came in and sat down he looked over at me and said something that sounded like 'How do you do?' I asked him if he was hungry and he shook his head 'yes.' His clothes were wet and he was very cold; in fact so cold he could not hold a knife and fork in his hands. His face was blue from the cold. I told my wife several days before if anyone came along and asked for food to give him all he wanted. The way she piled food on the table was a caution and the way he ate it was a greater caution. Why, I never saw a man with such a ravenous appetite. It seemed as if he couldn't stuff down his throat fast enough. All the time he was eating he was hurriedly looking about the room and glancing at both my wife and myself. He wasn't a bit nervous, but seemed in a hurry to finish. When he got through he thanked us for the meal and went out the same door he came in. He had a gunny sack with him, and before he left I picked it up. It only weighed a couple of pounds, and I think it contained some sacks which he used to sleep on.

When he came out from his meal he threw himself on a chair that was on the porch and rested a few minutes. He appeared worn out. He only sat down a few minutes, and, thanking me again, walked out of the front gate and went south about a quarter of a mile towards the school house.

Immediately after Blanck left, Nelson followed him and jumped behind a tree when he spotted Blanck checking out his hired man, who had passed the fugitive on the road. For a few minutes the jaded killer stood as if dazed and then took the road toward Orillia. Trailing Blanck, Nelson encountered Orillia grocer Bob Cameronu, and the two men pursued the fugitive in the grocer's wagon at a fast pace. Cameronu had a rifle, but did not attempt to use it when they caught up to Blanck. Continuing on until they were three-quarters of a mile from Orillia, Nelson got out, crossed a field and watched the road. When the hunted man failed to show up, Nelson went to Orillia and had the telegraph operator wire his counterpart in Kent that Blanck was headed that way.[1]

The word was quickly passed to two special deputies from Kent: forty-three-year-old Austrian native John Shepich, and Robert Crow, age twenty-one, whose father, J. J. Crow, was also a special deputy. The two men immediately grabbed a pair of .44-calibre Winchester rifles and hightailed it up the Northern Pacific railroad tracks.

As the two lawmen proceeded around a curve in the tracks three-quarters of a mile north of Kent at 4:40 p.m., they saw a man about 300 yards away in the middle of the tracks, plodding slowly towards them. His hat was pulled down over his eyes, his hands were by his side, and he gave no indication that he saw the two deputies. It was Tom Blanck.

When Blanck was less than thirty yards away, Shepich, who was in the lead, raised his rifle, aimed it at Blanck's heart, and called out, "Throw up your hands!" Making no effort to comply, Blanck slowly looked up and continued walking toward the two lawmen.

"Throw up your hands I tell you!" shouted Shepich. Blanck stopped, and in a dead, flat, faraway voice, the stupefied killer responded, "Well, what in hell do you want?" Blanck continued to stand as if he were in another world, his hands at his side. The now unnerved Shepich cried out a third time, "Up with those hands."

This brought the fugitive out of his reverie, and the embodiment of the dead-shot killer Tom Blanck was rekindled. With lightning speed, Blanck drew Yerbury's .38 from his hip pocket and, without seeming to aim, fired a deadly bullet directly at Shepich's heart. The lawman was fortunate, he had his arm up and the slug glanced off his wrist, entered his shoulder, broke his collarbone and stopped three inches above his heart near the scapula.

Blanck then neatly stepped off the tracks to his right and fired another shot at Shepich, narrowly missing him. Crow then entered the fight, shooting his Winchester wildly at Blanck. The killer turned and sent two slugs at his new adversary, the first passing within inches of his right side and the second barely grazing his left side. The two rattled lawmen now began shooting blindly at Blanck, who fired back, and the smoke rose in clouds.

Tom Blanck's luck was running out, and the first and only object of his love, his gun, now failed him. It was empty. He hurled himself down the embankment on the east side of the tracks and scuttled along the ground, concealing himself near a mound in the rushes.

In the lull, Shepich realized he was wounded and exclaimed to Crow, "My God, Bob, I'm done for." At this point another special deputy, Charley Newell, arrived, and was told by Shepich to drive the fugitive from his hiding place. Shepich then yelled at Blanck to come out.

Tom Blanck had no more options. His weapon was empty and he did not have the strength to escape or physically put up a fight. He undoubtedly was burning up with fever and nearly out on his feet. There was only one thing left to do. He laboriously rose to his feet, raised both hands in the air and walked toward the lawmen.

When Blanck reached the foot of the embankment, hands in the air and unarmed, Shepich said something to Crow. Then both men, with jagged nerves and adrenalin pumping, wildly blazed away, peppering the air with lead. Blanck immediately dropped to the ground and tried to crawl for cover. It did him no good, and the two special deputies, now joined by Newell, kept firing at the prostrate killer.

All in all, sixteen shots were fired by the lawmen and five by Blanck. Robert Crow's brother Thomas, also a posse man, arrived just as the shooting stopped, and he ran down the embankment and yanked Yerbury's gray fedora from Blanck's head. Crow stood there as Tom Blanck opened his mouth and gasped once, and then he watched as the killer's body relaxed in death.[2]

Shepich would later claim that during the exchange of gunfire he put an exploding bullet through the upper part of Blanck's right arm that exploded in the killer's lungs and exited out the center of his chest. Had that happened, it would have been impossible for Blanck to have walked out with both hands in the air. Also, if the bullet had exploded in Blanck's lungs, it would not have exited through his chest. Seven slugs hit Tom Blanck, but the postmortem examination proved without a doubt that the fatal shots were fired into Blanck's body when he was down.

One bullet undoubtedly hit Blanck while he was standing at the bottom of the embankment. It entered the lobe of his left ear and exited at the center of the back of his neck, searing a yellow streak across his back, indicating it was a downward shot. The bullet did not penetrate the brain and was not a fatal shot; however, the shot likely knocked him to the ground. The slug that Shepich claimed he fired during the first encounter entered Blanck's right arm at the shoulder, passed through the arm into his right lung and exited just above the right nipple. From the angle, this shot had to have been fired when Blanck was prone to the ground.

Three bullets hit Blanck in the back over his right lung and another entered the back part of his left shoulder. All lodged in his body. The first three were the killing shots, and all four were prevented from exiting by the protective blankets in the back of his coat. There was one other wound that conceivably could have hit Blanck while he was standing. It entered the right wrist and came out at the forearm. However, this is also improbable since Blanck had his hands in the air, unless a slug hit him during the gunfight. In either case, it was not a mortal wound. The angle of the fatal wounds prove that they had to have been fired downward into a prostrate body. Tom Blanck was executed.[3]

Later, the men in the posse would give the lame excuse that they

ROBERT CROW.

Artist's sketches of Robert Crow (above) and John Shepich (next page), the two men who killed Tom Blanck. From the *Seattle Post-Intelligencer.*

JOHN SHEPICH

thought Blanck, an empty-handed man with his hands in the air, had another gun. Graphically, the *Post-Intelligencer* gave an essentially accurate account:

> Hunger, loss of sleep and exhaustion must have shaken even his iron nerve, for although he was ready as ever with his gun his aim was not as true as in other encounters and he fired five shots, scoring only one hit.
>
> Game to the last, he never showed a sign of giving up until his last bullet was fired and until he was so badly wounded that he could no longer speak. Then he threw up his hands, but his captors, thinking he had mortally wounded one of them, determined to have life for life and continued the fusillade until he gasped out his last breath.[4]

Blanck's old friend George Howe likely summed it up best:

> Now that it is all over I don't know but that it is better for the poor fellow to be dead. I knew that he would never be taken alive as long as he had a shot in his pistol...I am satisfied that when Blanck approached the two men on the track he did not realize the condition he was in and believed he could kill one or both before they could fire on him.
>
> Anyone knows with a moment's thought that if he had killed Shepich he would have gotten his gun, removed the boy [Robert Crow] and gone down the track with two Winchester rifles, throwing death in all directions.[5]

When the shooting stopped, a crowd quickly gathered to look at the body of the noted gunman. Shepich turned to Tom Crow and exclaimed, "My God, Tom, get me to Kent as quickly as possible; I'm shot to death." Crow and posse man John S. Brown saw a section man with a handcar pumping like crazy trying to flee the scene of the shooting. When they called for him to return, he pumped all the faster. When they trained their rifles on him, he came back. Shepich was placed on the handcar and taken to Kent as fast as the car could go.

About halfway to Kent, another handcar with J. J. Crow and ex-policeman John Sandstrom aboard was met. The two removed their car from the tracks, allowing the wounded Shepich be taken to Kent. Back on the tracks, Crow and Sandstrom headed for the scene of the shooting. When they arrived, Blanck's body had been laid by the side of the tracks. A crowd was milling around discussing the identity of the dead man when Sanstrom walked up and looked at the body. The *Post-Intelligencer*, borrowing part of this phrase from the coroner, descriptively reported: "In the cold, white and ghastly upturned features he [Sanstrom] immediately recognized Thomas Blanck, the demon murderer and most desperate man ever brought to earth in this state by cold lead."[6]

[1] *Seattle Post-Intelligencer*, March 22, 23, 1895.

[2] *Seattle Post-Intelligencer*, March 22, 1895; *King County Coroner's Reports*, Vol. 2, p.9 (Thos. Blanck).

[3] *Seattle Post-Intelligencer*, March 22, April 25, 1895; Interview with Dr. Geraldine Powell (former pathologist), Ashville, North Carolina, July 7, 1992.

[4] *Seattle Post-Intelligencer*, March 22, 1895.

[5] *Seattle Post-Intelligencer*, March 29, 1895.

[6] *Seattle Post-Intelligencer*, March 22, 1895.

CHAPTER EIGHTEEN

A Dime Novel Hero

In death, Michael Hogan, Jr. alias Thomas Hamilton Blanck attained greater stature then he ever achieved in life. This is not an uncommon occurrence when someone dies. In Blanck's case, however, it was phenomenal as well as bizarre; through exaltation, Tom Blanck became a folk hero or, as William Pinkerton called him, a "dime-novel-reading desperado."

The question arises: why and how could a cold-blooded, remorseless killer gain such fame? The answers are found in the social, economic and political conditions that existed in the United States at the time.

Socially, Americans were, for the most part, members of isolated communities, receiving their news mainly from local newspapers. They followed them religiously and basically accepted what they read. To this end, the *Post-Intelligencer* has to take the blame for creating "the monster of the Pacific northwest." Their repeated references to Blanck as "the Jesse James of the Northwest" and his noted proficiency with a revolver intrigued the public, but the clincher was their repetitive hints, which were completely unfounded and untrue, that Tom Blanck was a train robber with ties to big-time train robbing gangs. This is how Tom Blanck became a folk hero, but not why he reached that plateau.

When Leland Stanford pounded in the gold-headed spike at Promontory Point on May 10, 1869, joining the Central Pacific and the Union Pacific Railroads, the fate of the small farmer and businessman and the laboring class was sealed. To reach this end, President Ulysses Grant's Republican administration gave railroad promoters 23 million acres of land and $64 million in easy loans.

From this point, big business became king, and a select few would earn the title of "robber barons."

In the east, the Tweed Ring in New York, a corrupt political combine headed by William Marcy Tweed, stole more than $200 million from that state while the Gas Ring, its counterpart in Philadelphia, was filching in that city. In Washington, D. C., Grant's cabinet and Congress were riddled with corruption, many connected with the Credit Mobilier Company, Union Pacific's construction company, which siphoned off $23 million from the U.S. Treasury. In 1873, Vice-President Schuyler Colfax squelched a probe into the company's activities after receiving bribes.

Also in 1873 came the Wall Street Panic, a depression that lasted six years. The major cause was the bankruptcy of robber baron Jay Cooke's banking firm, which overextended its promotion of the Northern Pacific Railway. More than 23,000 small businesses were wiped out. The only winners were the big corporations, which bought up the failed businesses for a song. The "crime of 1873" was Congress' passage of general revisions of the coinage laws demonetizing silver. A provision omitted silver from being freely coined, which reportedly was designed to injure the farmer and debtor classes in the west and south.

There was a national slump of farm prices: wheat fell from $1.50 to 67¢ a bushel, corn from 75¢ to 38¢ a bushel, and cotton from 31¢ to 9¢ a pound. The Grange, a secret society designed to act politically for farmers, was founded. They aimed their attacks on the railroad monopolies, who had initially brought in the small farmers and then charged them such excessive freight rates that profit was nonexistent. Many lost their farms, which were then taken over by the railroads, and the process was repeated.

In July, 1877, the Baltimore and Ohio Railroad cut wages by 10 percent-the third wage cut in as many years. Workers went on strike, and the Maryland militia marched on the strikers in Baltimore, fired on a hostile crowd and killed twelve people. The strike spread to Pittsburgh, where the Pennsylvania Railroad had also cut wages. Fifty-seven strikers and soldiers were killed and $3 million worth of railroad property was destroyed.

The 1880s were just as bad. Statements like, "Law? What do I care about law. Hain't I got the power?" from Cornelius Vanderbilt, and "The public be damned!" from Vanderbilt's son William Henry, helped fan the flames of dissent. In 1887, the Farmer's Alliance was formed to improve farming conditions through social and legislative actions. This movement evolved into the Populist Party. After years of complaints against the railroads, Congress reluctantly created the Interstate Commerce Commission in 1887, a government board created to regulate private business and prevent rate discrimination. However, railroad lawyers and the federal courts hampered it so effectively that by 1895 it was all but extinct. On top of this, the severe droughts and blizzards of 1886–87 brought the small western farmers and ranchers to their knees.

The "Gay Nineties" was a misnomer, and reform was just as ineffective as it had been the previous two decades. In 1890, Congress passed the Anti-Trust Act, geared to prohibit monopolies from restraining free trade. Adverse court actions rendered it impotent. The Billion Dollar Congress of 1890 paid off big business by raising tariffs, which raised freight rates, which in turn raised consumer prices and brought an immense outcry throughout the entire country. People saw the government in bed with big business and demonstrated their aversion to government from the federal level on down.

In the off election year of 1890, the Populists reached their zenith. They stood on a platform that asserted that organized big business, especially the railroads, were sucking the country dry through monopoly prices, exorbitant railroad rates and tariffs. The election wrecked the Billion Dollar Congress, and Republicans were swept out of power. The new House had 235 Democrats, many of whom were tinged with Populism, as opposed to 88 Republicans.

The population of the U.S. in 1900 was 63 million people, and 11 million out of 12 million families were living on $380 a year. In 1893, the U.S. suffered another depression, which President Grover Cleveland blamed on the 1890 Silver Purchase Act that had allotted gold be used to buy silver while the rest of the world was on the gold standard. The farmers and silverites opposed his efforts to maintain the gold standard. As a result, there was less circulating money in 1890 than when the Civil War ended in 1865, even though the population had doubled and business had tripled.

By 1894, the common man had reached rock bottom. The depression took its toll. Laid off railroad workers in the west trudged their way east, threatening to march on the capitol. As many as 750,000 went out on strike, essentially for higher wages. The act that broke the camel's back had occurred in late 1893, when the Pullman Palace Car Company took advantage of the depression, laid off most of its employees and hired them back at wage cuts up to 25 percent. The workers went on strike, and in May, 1894, President Cleveland ordered regular army troops to Chicago to enforce a federal injunction against strikers. In the end, twelve strikers were killed and the strike was broken. These conditions would plague the American people for nearly twenty more years.

The views people in the state of Washington held concerning the railroads were no different than those maintained by their counterparts throughout the rest of the United States. According to author Robert E. Ficken: "Just a few years earlier, the Northern Pacific and other railroad lines had been welcomed into the developing region as they promised to forge transportation links to eastern markets, to open land, and to bring in population and myriad blessings. But after a few years such promises turned sour. Railroad moguls flirted callously with places seeking service or selection as terminus points and held entire communities hostage to exorbitant rate structures. The rhetoric of disaffected farmers blasted the influence of railroads on the economy and on people's lives."[1]

A decade later, Canadians in Victoria, British Columbia, the neighboring big city to Seattle, summed up very well the people's consensus of railroad companies. Bill Miner, an old-time stagecoach and train robber, had been convicted for train robbery, and the popular joke was, "Oh, Bill Miner is not so bad, he only robs the CPR [Canadian Pacific Railroad] once every two years, but the CPR robs us every day."[2] These sentiments give a good indication as to how Tom Blanck became a folk hero. The *Post-Intelligencer* should never have insinuated that he was a train robber.

Even before his spectacular jailbreak, Tom Blanck had begun to acquire a folk hero's mantle. When William Pinkerton visited the jail in King County, he made these comments when asked about Blanck by a reporter. They were pretty much on the mark:

> Judging from what I have read of him in the POST-INTELLI-GENCER, he is a dime-novel-reading desperado, more fool than knave. He has no appreciation of the value of human life, and would kill a man for $2 as readily as he would for $2,000.

At any rate, he is a commonplace criminal, and far from being the hero that many people have painted him from the reports published of him.[3]

Regardless, the people bestowed upon Tom Blanck the hero's mantle. Deep in their minds, they likely knew he was not what they desired him to be, but he was all they had. They could see an image of a dime novel gunman like Wild Bill Hickok, but more importantly they saw, or wanted to see, a man in the shade of Jesse James, a symbol of resistance and retaliation against both governmental authority and their common foe-the railroad. The state of Washington and the city of Seattle would now paid homage to their dead "hero," and it became a three-ring circus.

[1] Mark Dugan, *The Making Of Legends*, pp.1-3; George Brown Tindall, *America, A Narrative History,* pp.730-31, 782-84, 876-81, 885-94; Roger Butterfield, *The American Past*, pp.224-25, 226-27, 234-35, 244-45, 254, 258-59, 266-67; Robert E. Ficken, *Washington: A Centennial History,* pp.74-75.

[2] Mark Dugan and John Boessenecker, *The Grey Fox, The True Story Of Bill Miner, Last Of The Old-Time Bandits*, p.130.

[3] *Seattle Post-Intelligencer*, October 25, 1894.

CHAPTER NINETEEN

"No Dead Criminal Received the Attention Thomas Blanck Did"

"It's Tom Blanck, sure, and we might as well take his body to Kent," said John Sandstrom as he looked down at the dead gunman just minutes after the killing. When J. J. Crow and Sandstrom arrived at the depot in Kent they found the whole town had turned out to see the dead killer. The corpse was carried into the waiting room and laid on a bench where the crowd gazed at the bloody wounds in the notorious gunman's body.

A wire was immediately sent to Sheriff Van de Vanter, who was ten miles down the track. He telegraphed back to have the body ready to transport to Seattle, and he boarded the train for Kent. When the train reached the station, the sheriff pushed his way into the waiting room and had Blanck's body placed into the baggage car where deputies McDonald, Cave, and Pauley were waiting to view the remains of the man who had eluded them for four days. Receiving congratulations from the officers, Robert Crow climbed aboard with Van de Vanter, and the train pulled out for Seattle.

The news spread quickly throughout Seattle, and a vast throng of people hurried to the station to beat the train. When it arrived at 7:30 p.m., the sheriff poked his head out of the baggage car and saw this huge, shouting mob milling around the depot. Just moments before the train pulled in, a patrol wagon had thundered into the station and twelve policemen tumbled out to control the rowdy crowd.

Funeral Home owner Edgar Ray Butterworth, in the funeral home office around the time of Tom Blanck's funeral. *Courtesy Bert Butterworth, Seattle.*

Six of the policemen climbed into the baggage car, a coffin was shoved in and Blanck's body was placed inside. When four of the men started to carry the coffin to the dead wagon, the mob started screaming and shouting; the policemen had to literally use their clubs to keep them back. When the dead wagon headed for the morgue, the throng followed closely behind.

By the time Blanck's body was taken inside the morgue, a large crowd had already gathered to see the remains, among them were Detectives Cudihee and Corbett. When the sheet was removed from the dead man's face, Cudihee was so overwhelmed he sympathetically exclaimed, "My God, how tired he looks. The poor fellow was evidently completely worn out."

The *Post-Intelligencer* described the dead killer's condition: "Blanck's face was thin and weariness, loss of sleep and extreme

NAME OF DECEASED Alias "Thomas Blanck"   Ordered by Dr. O. P. Aakam. Coroner

Address,   Relationship, none

Place of death, Near O'Brien and Kent   Persons calling,

Previous Residence, County Jail   Bill Made to King County

Place of Birth,   Bill Rendered or Mailed to   Date, 4/1 '95

Birthplace of Father,   of Mother,   Certifying Physician, Dr. Aakam

Single, Married, Widow, Widower,   Male or Female,   Cause of Death, Shot by Crow Jobepich Deputy Sheriff

Age, 24 Yrs.   Mos.   Days   Size   Ft.   Place of Burial, Duwamish Cem.

Occupation, Coalminer   In.   Grave or Lot,

Date of Death, Mar 21, 95   Place of Shipment,

Date of Funeral, " 25, "   Shipped by

Services held at Parlor   Rmark, Shot 6 times in head and body.

Services held by 0   He was the murderer of Marshal Jeffreys of

Date of Shipment,   Puyallup and of Chas Bradwell of

Previous Burials,   Seattle and 5 or more others.

CHARGE TO

Person Responsible, King County   Relationship,

Address—Residence,   Business,

No.   Plate Engraved.   No.   Handles,

Hearse to Cemetery,

Carriages to Cemetery,

Carriages to

Washing and laying out Remains, Shaving, Dressing,

Preserving Remains by

Crepe for Pall Bearers,

Pairs of   Gloves

Use of Door Drapery,

Outside Box, sent to Cemetery on

Opening Grave in Lot,

Advertising Funeral in

Payments, $13 00

April 8 by cash King Co. $13 00

Record of Tom Blanck's funeral, showing the costs of $13.00 being paid by King
County. E. R. Butterworth and Sons Funeral Records, 1895. *Courtesy Butterworth
Manning Ashmore, Funeral Directors, Seattle.*

hunger were written in every line of his countenance. He was wet through from rain and must have suffered greatly from the cold while in the swamp between Renton and O'Brien."

Shortly after 8:00 p.m., Coroner O. P. Askam and Dr. Gibson conducted a postmortem examination. Both medical men concluded that Blanck died instantly from the shots that entered his back while in a prone position. They reported that the dead killer's lungs were full of "pigment inhalations" of coal dust with "little black spots appearing all through the lungs." From this they assumed Blanck was a coal miner. They also stated he was suffering the first stages of pneumonia and gave a graphic portrait of Tom Blanck to a reporter: "He was not a massive man by any means, but was strong and sinewy and the physicians say they never saw a man more perfectly built, and from the waist down he looked more like a woman than a man. His arms were well developed and he had a magnificent chest, and he very likely could run like a greyhound and also, when necessary, he could put up a telling hand-to-hand fight. It was the opinion of the physicians that he did not look like a confirmed criminal, and he did not have a scar on his body except the holes that were put in him when killed."

Coroner Askam told reporters that an inquest would be held the following afternoon at E. R. Butterworth and Sons' undertaking rooms. Indicating it did not matter how Blanck died, he added, "It will be a sort of formal proceeding to exonerate the men who did the county and state a great service." Following the postmortem, Blanck's body was taken to Butterworth's and embalmed.[1]

The coroner also filled out two King County death records. On the Death Register, Askam listed the cause of death, "Shot while resisting arrest." The Death Record was another matter; whether through humor or abhorrence, likely a little of both, Askam unprecedentedly ascribed the cause of death as "Cold Lead," the phrase that was used the next day by the *Post-Intelligencer*.[2]

The following day at Butterworth's, a six-man coroner's jury found, "That the said Shepich and Crow were seeking to arrest him under the authority of the Sheriff of King Co. and that the said Thos. Blanck resisted by firing at them with a revolver. We find the killing of Blanck justifiable."[3]

It was at Butterworth's undertaking rooms on Pine Street that the idolization of Tom Blanck was manifested. The *Post-*

9

Name of Deceased *Thos Blanck* No. 9

Date of Death *March 21st 1895* Age *24 yrs.*

Residence *Seattle* Occupation

Personal Description *Light complexion, brown hair – small light mustache, blue eyes – Height 5 ft. 9½ in – Weight about 160 lbs*

Cause of Death *Shot, while resisting arrest –*

Date of Inquest or Investigation *March 22nd 1895*

Result of Inquest or Investigation *We, the undersigned, the Jurors summoned to appear before C.P. Askam Coroner of King Co. Wash. at Seattle, in said Co. & State on 22nd day of March, 1895 to inquire into the death of Thos. Blanck who was killed in said Co. Mch. 21, 1895 having been duly sworn according to law & having made inquisition after inspecting the body & hearing the testimony adduced on our oath, each & all do say, that we find the name of deceased was Thos. Blanck age about 24 yrs. nativity unknown. That he came to his death on 21st Mch. 1895 about 4:40 P.M. 9½ mi. N. of Kent on N.P.R.R. Track from gun-shot wounds inflicted by John Shepich & Robert E. Crow. We find that Thos Blanck was a desperate criminal under sentence of death for murder, who had recently escaped from the Jail of King Co. & was known to be armed. That the said Shepich & Crow were seeking to arrest him under the authority of the Sheriff of King Co. & that the said Thos Blanck resisted by firing at them with a revolver. We find the killing of Blanck was justifiable*

		Fees and Mileage	$	
Foreman	*Lester Turner*			2 20
Juror	*Wm Boyd*	" " "		2 20
"	*Ed. Terby*	" " "		2 20
"	*W. M. Slater*	" " "		2 20
"	*G. O. Guess*	" " "		2 20
"	*W. R. Forrest*	" " "		2 20
Witness	*A. T. Van de Vanter*	" " "		.2 20
"	*R. E. Crow*	" " "		2 20
"	*Thos. Crow*	" " "		2 20
"		" " "		
"		" " "		
"		" " "		

Coroner's Report on the death of Tom Blanck. King County Coroner's Reports, Vol. 2. *Courtesy King County Archives, Seattle, Washington.*

Intelligencer vividly described the opening scene at Butterworth's on the twenty-second: "The street in front of the undertaking rooms was crowded all day from early morn until evening, and so great was the pressure on the doors, despite the efforts of five policemen, the public was admitted long before the intended time. Almost as many women as men took advantage of the opportunity to get a look at the greatest of Pacific Northwest criminals."[4]

From Thursday night, March 21, until Monday, March 25, Blanck's body was exhibited on a slab at the funeral home. Although an actual count of viewers was never taken, an estimate can be garnered from *Post-Intelligencer* reports, unless the press engaged in sensationalism. If the reports were factual, or even just close to the facts, the outcome was staggering.

142

DEATH RECORD.

No.	Date of Death	NAME	Age	Occupation	Where Born	Place of Death	CAUSE OF DEATH Primary	Incomplete

DEATH RECORD

Duration of Disease	Sex	Color	Married, Single, Widow, Widower	Place of Interment	Attending Physician	REMARKS

King County, Washington Death Record, showing the coroner denoting "Cold Lead" as the cause of death of Tom Blanck. *Courtesy Division of Archives and Records Management, Olympia, Washington.*

No count was reported for Thursday night, but from the huge crowd that was on hand likely 2,500 people saw Blanck's body. On Friday, the twenty-second, in a one half-hour period, 1,500 people came to see the dead desperado. From 11:00 a.m. until closing at 9:00 p.m., the lowest estimate of onlookers was 18,000. It is probable that around 24,000 people flooded through the funeral home that first day. There was no count taken the next day, but on the twenty-fifth the *Post-Intelligencer* reported, "The body has been lying in 'state' since Thursday night and as yet the morbid curiosity of the crowd has not been satisfied." This indicates the numbers were high, and since it was a Saturday, the number may have been as high as 25,000 people. On Sunday morning, the twenty-fourth, 2,300 viewed the dead gunman. This is the lowest amount of people reported, but maybe they were at church. Being conservative, the numbers by that night might have climbed to 10,000. There was no report for the morning of the twenty-fifth, but if the newspaper was right, another 5,000 could be reasonably added.

Taking the newspaper reports as a guideline, the total number that likely came to see Tom Blanck's body was a staggering 66,000 people; the entire population of Seattle in 1890 was about 42,000. A substantiating fact that this inordinate number of people viewed the dead killer was that by the twenty-fifth the rug at Butterworth's was completely worn out, and the padding was virtually gone. It was undoubtedly the largest service the bewildered Edgar Ray Butterworth ever had. Yet this story grows more fascinating.

On the twenty-third, a somewhat baffled *Post-Intelligencer* reporter wrote: "Great interest seems to attach itself to everything the late desperado, Tom Blanck, ever owned, and crowds will stand for hours and look at anything he possessed. Today the big display window of Hyams, Pauson & Co. will contain a form dressed in the clothing which Blanck wore when he was suddenly called to his long home. A life-sized portrait of Blanck will be placed in the window, together with the gun he took away from Night Jailer Yerbury...."

Tom Blanck even became the subject of a church sermon. On the Sunday morning following Blanck's death, Dr. Allison spoke to his congregation about the life and death of Blanck, beginning his sermon with "Poor Blanck." There was no report about how it was received.

From the time Blanck's body was put on exhibition, his enchanted public displayed their admiration of him with actions, not words. Within the astounding numbers of people who viewed Blanck's body, there was a significant number who adorned their "hero's" bier with flowers. The most blatant display of affection was bizarre; women would lean over and kiss the dead killer's face. The *Post-Intelligencer* would incredulously state, "No dead criminal, however noted he may have been, has ever received the attention that the body of Thomas Blanck did..."[5]

On the day Blanck was killed, Sheriff Hagen and Marshal Stevens captured Willie Holmes near Sultan City. Charles Williams was captured on the twenty-fourth after being spotted on a train at Leavenworth, Washington. R. H. "Smoke House Kid" Ford ran right into the clutches of Detective Cudihee and Chief Rogers in Seattle during the afternoon of March 23. The first thing Ford asked was to allow him to see the body of his dead mentor. Wanting to duck a large crowd that had gathered, the two officers granted his request. His reactions were recorded in the *Post-Intelligencer*, "As Ford stood looking at the corpse, it was observed that he was deeply moved, but he made no remarks and walked out with his captors in deep silence."[6]

This idolization of Tom Blanck cannot be attributed solely to the public's reaction to social, political and economic conditions. Blanck himself had a lot to do with it. The mystery surrounding his background piqued the public's interest; even his lawyer was intrigued. The fact that the authorities and the newspapers could only speculate, then create and, finally, sensationalize some of his background added fuel to the fire. His alias of Blanck was a contributory factor, and the killer likely chose it to mock the authorities, who certainly did draw a blank when they investigated him. Back again to the *Post-Intelligencer*, who fed it to the public, and the public ate it up.

As with all noted desperados, rumors began to circulate that the dead man at Butterworth's was not Tom Blanck. It raised the ire of Chief Rogers who declared challengingly, "This report is too ridiculous to be considered! It is Blanck without a doubt." The *Post-Intelligencer* checked it out with the authorities and reported: "Ex-Sheriff J. H. Woolery said there could not be any mistake as to the identity. Jailer Monroe laughed when he heard the story, and said he

Edward Cudihee around the time he was elected to serve a second term as sheriff of King County, Washington in 1913. *Author's collection.*

ought to know 'Tom' when he saw him. Ex-City Detective John Roberts, who had the fight in the court house with Blanck at the time of the trial, said he knew it was Blanck. The same conviction was echoed by Detective Cudihee, City Jailer Peer, Special Deputy Sheriff Dick Burkman, Police Clerk Kennedy, who registered Blanck when he was first caught, ex-Deputy United States Marshal E. V. Rugar, Detective Gil Philbrick and I. N. Hooper." The newspaper referred to the rumor as wild, and pointed out that the jail keys and Yerbury's revolver that Blanck took were found with the dead man.[7]

Crazy things happened too. A man who professed to be a phrenologist examined Blanck's head on the twenty-third and said Blanck did not possess one redeeming trait. The next day a Mrs. Shaw of Fremont, Washington, walked into Butterworth's and told the staff to put off the burial of Blanck as she believed he was a friend's husband that had disappeared into the woods a week before. The newspaper called it absurd, and Butterworth's ignored the woman's ridiculous claim. Another woman said Blanck looked like her husband, and a distorted story quickly circulated around Seattle that a woman had claimed the dead man was her husband and not Tom Blanck.[8]

On Saturday, Coroner Askam stated that Blanck's body would be buried on the following Monday in the potter's field, and so it was. Tom Blanck's funeral was an anticlimax to the exhibition at Butterworth's the previous four days. Apparently none of his admirers attended, and no newspaper bothered to report it. The adulation bestowed on the killer was buried with him. The fickle public had no use for a dead desperado six feet underground, and they promptly forgot him.

The burial was held on the twenty-fifth, and Tom Blanck was unceremoniously dumped into a pauper's grave in the Duwamish Cemetery, commonly called potter's field, on the grounds of the King County Hospital, the county "poor farm." In 1970, Dr. Kenneth Sherwood wrote, "On the 11th of May 1877, the Sisters [of Providence] took possession of the county "Poor House" and King County Hospital was officially open. This Poor House was a modest two story frame building 50 by 60 feet in size, located in Georgetown on the banks of the Duwamish River." Evidently Tom Blanck's only mourners were the gravediggers and whoever represented Butterworth's. The funeral bill of thirteen dollars was paid by the county in cash on April 8.[9]

In the aftermath, a forty-dollar fund that had been collected for Cudihee and Corbett for the capture of Blanck was refused by the two officers on the grounds that the capture was made in the line of duty, so special badges were made for the two lawmen. Blanck's capture enhanced Edward Cudihee's reputation, and he was elected twice to serve four-year terms as sheriff of King County, first in 1901 and again in 1913. In 1902, Cudihee led the great manhunt for Harry Tracy; however, he was not as lucky as he had been with Tom Blanck and was always one step behind the elusive Tracy. Sheriff A. T. Van de Vanter also benefited from his intense manhunt for Tom Blanck, and was reelected as sheriff in 1899.

Farmer James Nelson, who fed Blanck his last meal, filed a claim for the $500-reward for Blanck. On April 18, the King County Commissioners disallowed Nelson's claim, but awarded John Shepich $333.34, and Robert Crow, $166.66. All in all, 111 men received pay on April 17 for serving as special deputies.[10]

[1] *Seattle Post-Intelligencer*, March 22, 1895.

[2] *King County Death Register*, Record No. 1484, Blanck, Thos., March 21, 1895, p.19; *King County Death Record*, No. 131, Thomas Blanck, March 21, 1895, p.29.

[3] *King County Coroner's Reports*, Vol. 2, p.9 (Thos. Blanck).

[4] *Seattle Post-Intelligencer*, March 23, 1895.

[5] *Seattle Post-Intelligencer*, March 23, 25, 1895; The 1890 population of Seattle was 42,837 according to information from the Division of Archives and Records Management, Olympia, Washington.

[6] *Seattle Post-Intelligencer*, March 22, 24, 25, 1895.

[7] *Seattle Post-Intelligencer*, March 24, 1895.

[8] *Seattle Post-Intelligencer*, March 24, 25, 1895.

[9] E. R. Butterworth and Sons Funeral Records, 1895, Alias "Thomas Blanck," p.124. Butterworth Manning Ashmore, Funeral Directors, Seattle; Kenneth W. Sherwood, M.D. *The Development of King County Hospital*, n.p.

[10] *Seattle Post-Intelligencer*, March 24, April 25, 1895; Information on the Sheriffs of King County provided by the Department of Public Safety, King County Sheriff's Department, King County Courthouse, Seattle; *Journal Of Proceedings Of County Commissioners, King County, Washington*, Volume 9, pp.172, 210-13.

Chapter Twenty

The Final Mystery

Following the death of Tom Blanck, two puzzling questions remain unanswered. First, why was his true identity as Michael Hogan never revealed in Seattle? Montana and New York had this information, and reportedly received it from Seattle. Blanck confessed his true identity to George Howe, who in turn told Jailer W. T. Monroe. The *Evening Star* in Blanck's hometown of Schenectady reported, "The confession was corroborated by the jailer [Monroe] by a telegram received from City Marshal Davis of Helena, Montana..." Did Howe or Monroe pass this information to an out-of-state reporter and not to the *Post-Intelligencer*? Regardless, Schenectady's two newspapers obtained the information and printed it. One can only speculate.

This leads to another question: did Michael Hogan, Jr.'s parents and siblings learn of his notoriety and fate? This seems probable, for the killer not only made the news in Schenectady, his notoriety gained him a shot in the *New York Times*.[1] If his family did read about him, none of them made any effort to either contact the authorities in Seattle for more information or bring his body back to New York for burial. They likely considered it good riddance.

If the above piques one's curiosity, the following is simply unexplainable, as well as ironic. In November and December of 1912, more than seventeen years after Tom Blanck's death, all the bodies in potter's field were reportedly exhumed. The Duwamish Cemetery, or potter's field, was one of the earliest cemeteries in the Seattle area and was used primarily as an Indian and pauper burial site. According to *A Directory of Cemeteries and Funeral Homes in Washington State*: "This cemetery was operated by the King County Hospital and Poor Farm, which overlooked the Duwamish River.

Register *Total received from Cemetery.* 1912.

Reg. NO.	NAMES	Holder No.	Date Billed	Amount
50	855 having names dates & on headboards			
51				
52	493 having only numbers on headboards			
53				
54	1912 having no mark, either numbers or name			
55	" and no headboards.			
56				
57				
58	As above stated 3260 remains of			
59	bodies exhumed from King County			
60	potters field, during the months			
61	of November and December 1912.			
62	were delivered at County Crematory			
63	and cremated, with the exception			
64	of one which was removed to			
65	Pleasant View Cemetery.			
66				
67	Attest			
68	G.B. Arnold			
69	Caretaker.			
70				

Page from the *Potter's Field Record Book* confirming the exhumation and cremation of the remains of 3,259 bodies in the Duwamish Cemetery in 1912.

Two acres were set aside in 1873 as a public cemetery. One of the earliest burials was in 1876."[2]

By 1912, Seattle was expanding and the site on which potter's field was located was needed for development. In the summer of 1912, the King County Crematorium was erected on the King

County Hospital grounds, and on November 13, 1912, the King County Board of Commissioners passed an order that all bodies in potter's field be exhumed and cremated. One of the resolutions read, "the ashes shall be retained in a receptacle...and said ashes shall be retained in the Crematorium for at least two years." On a motion it was ordered "that the allowance of $10.00 to undertakers for burial of pauper dead, be discontinued, and that all pauper bodies hereafter be cremated at the King County Crematorium." All expenses were to be rendered to the Board of County Commissioners.

Following the exhumation and cremation of the remains, this report was filed by Cemetery Caretaker G. B. Arnold:

Total received from cemetery [year] 1912

855 having names dates on headboards.

493 having only numbers on headboards.

1912 having no mark, either numbers or names and no head-boards.

As above stated 3260 remains of bodies exhumed from King County potter's field, during the months of November and December 1912, were delivered at County Crematorium and cremated with the exception of one which was removed to Pleasant View Cemetery.

What happened to the remains of 3,259 bodies, including Tom Blanck's, whose grave was one of the 1,912 having no name, number or headboard?[3] This was an important and newsworthy decision by the Board of Commissioners, yet, throughout November of 1912, not one word about this was printed in Seattle's major newspaper, the *Post-Intelligencer*. Also, there are no known existing county or city records that reveal the final disposition of these remains.

It is rumored as an "open secret" in the Seattle area that the Board of Commissioners kept the whole affair quiet and, to save money, had all the bodies dumped in the Duwamish River. The lack of newspaper coverage/publicity and public records substantiating the cemetery caretaker's initial report adds more intrigue to the whole affair. Also, since all the remains were of paupers, there was no one to launch an investigation. However, this is a stretch, for surely some of these bodies would have washed ashore and eventually been discovered, which would have undoubtedly made headline news.

The *Beginnings, Progress and Achievement in the Medical Work of King County, Washington* states, "All remains were reduced to ashes and filed in the columbarium." Another report from the *History of Seattle Cemeteries*, which is unconfirmed and undocumented, claims that the remains were reinterred in the Comet Lodge Cemetery, also known as the Georgetown Cemetery, an Odd Fellows cemetery located in the South Beacon Hill area. In agreement, *A Directory of Cemeteries and Funeral Homes in Washington State* states, "In November 1912, 3,260 burials were exhumed and cremated, then reinterred," but the directory does not give the reinterment site. In 1987, someone claiming ownership reportedly bulldozed part of the Comet Lodge Cemetery, and many of the graves are no longer marked. However, records of the Comet Lodge Cemetery give no indication that the bodies were reinterred in that cemetery.[4]

After checking with several funeral homes and cemetery officials, it can be reasonably concluded that 3,259 bodies could not be cremated between the months of November and December of 1912, a period of a scant two months, and to dispose of that many bodies by dumping them into the Duwamish River stretches the imagination. Quoting Jerry Townsend of Bass & Smith Funeral Home in Hickory, North Carolina, who has forty-four years' experience in the funeral business, "There is no way they could dig up that many bodies and cremate them in that length of time, especially in that time period when the bodies would have to be dug up by hand. This would be virtually impossible at a time when the rule of law was that all graves were to be six feet deep." The only reference to this conundrum can be found in the *Annual Report of the King County Hospital For Year Ending December 31, 1917*, which, being unaware, fortuitously repudiates its own claim. The following is the article in full, titled "King County Crematory":

The King County Crematory is under the direct supervision of the business management of the King County Hospital. It was built

Map of the area of South Beacon Hill area of Seattle where the Duwamish and Georgetown Cemeteries are located and marked "D" and "G" respectively.

and put in operation during the year 1912, the first work done being the cremating of bodies which were exhumed during the months of November and December, 1912, from the Potter's Field. The number of these bodies was 3,260. The actual expense of cremation up to February 27, 1913, we are unable to state, as this office was not keeping record of the business at that time.; but

King County Hospital (Poor Farm) in 1917. The Duwamish Cemetery was located on the hospital grounds. *Courtesy Seattle, Washington Public Library.*

King County Hospital (Poor Farm) in 1932. Courtesy Seattle, Washington Municipal Archives.

The Duwamish Cemetery was located near this area, with the King County Hospital (Poor Farm) in the background. *Courtesy Seattle, Washington Municipal Archives.*

the approximate cost, I think, we could safely say would be about $3.561/2 each. This would include the exhuming, delivery of the bodies to the crematory and the cremating of bodies.

The records of the County Auditor's office show the original cost of installation of the King County Crematory to be $14,543.41. The building is built of brick, very neat in appearance. The main or front entrance opens into the chapel, which has a seating capacity of from two to three hundred people. From the chapel is an entrance to the cremating room, which is practically large enough to accommodate all who would wish to see a cremation. In this room are the retorts (two in number) for cremation. Each retort is large enough to accommodate two bodies, but for all practical purposes we prefer putting one body in each retort as the cremation can be done at less expense and in less time. The average time for cremating is from fifty to sixty minutes.

One factor the report left out is the down time the retort needs to cool off in order to remove the ashes. Today that time frame is about four hours. Using the figures this report gives, and adding in the down time, and supposing the crematory ran a full twenty-four

The old portion of the Comet Lodge Cemetery, also known as the Georgetown Cemetery, an Odd Fellows cemetery located in the South Beacon Hill area of Seattle where by some reports the bodies from the Duwamish Cemetery, including that of Tom Blanck, were reinterred. Photo taken in 2001 by Andi McDonald, Port Orchard, Washington. *Author's collection.*

hours a day for the time period reported (November 13 through December, 1912), which rounded off would be a generous fifty days, the total would be six bodies per day (one body per every four hours for twenty-four hours) times fifty which equals a maximum of 300 bodies. This still leaves a total of 2,959 bodies unaccounted for. Added evidence comes from the *Annual Report of the King County Hospital For Year Ending December 31, 1918*, which reported that only 286 bodies were cremated for the entire year of 1917 and 312 bodies cremated for the entire year of 1918. The probable solution to this enigma is that the remains of Tom Blanck and his fellow paupers were never removed and lie today where they were initially interred. Who was to complain?[5]

So, in the end, the vision of Tom Blanck's mocking smile comes back to haunt us all. In death he accomplished what he could not do in life—he made his escape, and this time it was forever.

[1] *Evening Star*, March 23, 1895; *Daily Union*, March 26, 30, 1895; *New York Times*, April 3, 1895.

[2] *A Directory of Cemeteries and Funeral Homes in Washington State*, p.128; Letter, dated July 13, 1992, Richard Engeman, University of Washington Libraries at Seattle, to author. There is confusion over the original location of the Duwamish Cemetery, which also has been mistaken for the Comet Lodge Cemetery. The Duwamish Cemetery, or potter's field, was located on the west side of Corson Avenue S, just north of S. Michigan Street. The Comet Lodge Cemetery, or Georgetown Cemetery, is located on 23 Avenue S and S. Graham.

[3] *Potter's Field Record Book, Cemetery Records*, 1912, 0.1 c.f., p.16. Seattle-King County Department of Health, Seattle; *Beginnings, Progress and Achievement in the Medical Work of King County, Washington*, p.55.

[4] *Beginnings, Progress and Achievement in the Medical Work of King County, Washington*, p.55; *History of Seattle Cemeteries*, provided by Dave Daly, President of Evergreen-Washelli (Cemeteries and Funeral Home), Seattle, Washington; *A Directory of Cemeteries and Funeral Homes in Washington State*, pp.116, 128; *Comet Lodge Cemetery Legal History; Comet Lodge Cemetery Burial List*.

[5] Interview with Mr. Jerry Townsend, Bass & Smith Funeral Home, Hickory, North Carolina, October 10, 2002; *Annual Report of the King County Hospital For Year Ending December 31, 1917*, p.36, and *Annual Report of the King County Hospital For Year Ending December 31, 1918*, p.12, listed under the *Biennial Report Of The King County Hospital*, 1917-1918.

Epilogue

"I have never been in love but once, and that was with a gun I had." This declaration by Tom Blanck undoubtedly echoes his true feelings, taking into consideration his animosity toward women. There are those in this world who continually go from one disastrous love affair to another, always to be let down. Tom Blanck was no exception, only in his case it was with revolvers. There were four known occasions where Tom Blanck's *affaire d'amour* with his gun went awry. All four can be attributed to choice.

The initial instance was the scene of Blanck's first known homicide in Weiser, Idaho. Following the accidental killing of his pal Sweeney in March, 1890, Blanck disgustedly tossed his revolver away during his escape. The *Weiser Leader* reported: "On Wednesday morning, while Harrison Jones' little boy, Johnnie, was playing back of Jones and Moore's blacksmith shop, he found a 44 calibre, double action six shooter on the roof of T. D. Flynn's old shed. The gun is one of the best manufacture, it contained five empty shells and one loaded cartridge that was dented as if it had snapped and missed fire. This is supposed to be the gun that the unknown man used in killing James Sweeny [sic] in this place several weeks ago, as it was found near where this man lost his hat in his flight."[1]

Blanck was probably disgusted and angry for two reasons: the revolver misfired and he missed his target, Judge Hanthorn, so he threw it away. The newspaper stated it was a double-action .44-calibre revolver made by one of the best manufacturers. This indicates the gun was likely a Smith and Wesson 44 Double Action First Model Revolver, also called the New Model Navy Number 3 and the Double Action Frontier, a popular revolver made from 1881 to 1913. A problem Blanck likely encountered was that double-action revolvers had a harder trigger pull than single-action models, and

Smith and Wesson .44 caliber Double Action First Model Revolver.

this may have pulled him off target. Since this was not a cheap "throw away," it brings back Howe's statement that Blanck would discard anything he had no more use for.[2]

Blanck's next experience with misguided love occurred in September, 1894, in Butte, Montana, when he repeatedly pulled the trigger of his revolver in an attempt to kill his robbery victim, Major Camp. His "loved one" let him down again, misfiring every time. This revolver was never described, but if the inefficiency of the fir-

Colt Single Action Army Revolver known as the "Peacemaker," produced in .44 and .45 calibers.

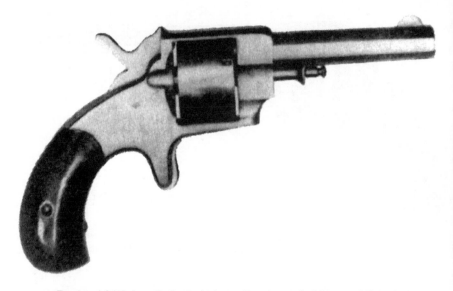

Forehand & Wadsworth Center Hammer Revolver, a "suicide special" marked BULLDOZER in .38 caliber and SWAMP ANGEL in .41 caliber.

ing mechanism was the cause of the misfiring, it may have been a cheap "bulldog" type revolver, commonly known throughout the next three decades as a "Suicide Special." Today they are called "Saturday Night Specials." These spur-triggered, low quality, small revolvers that used metallic cartridges were mass produced in the latter nineteenth and early twentieth century and could be bought inexpensively from various catalogs. Some of the colorful names were Bang Up, Bulldozer, Dead Shot, Earthquake, Paralyzer, Swamp Angel and Tramp's Terror.[3]

On the other hand, the fault may have been defective cartridges. By 1894, Blanck's proficiency with a revolver was well established, and he reportedly carried two revolvers, one a .44 calibre and the other a .45 calibre. One of these undoubtedly was the object of his one and only love. The gun he was using when arrested by Cudihee and Corbett was a single-action, .45-calibre Colt. It is probable that Blanck picked this type revolver for more accuracy, having a softer trigger pull. Another plausible reason was that this was the most famous and popular revolver of the American frontier, a standard for shooters. The Colt Single Action Army Revolver, commonly known

Brooklyn Arms Co.— Slocum Front-Loading Revolver, another "suicide special" in .32 caliber.

as the Peacemaker, was produced from 1872 until 1940. A total of 357,859 revolvers were manufactured.[4]

Tom Blanck's final recipient of his adoration would not only fail and disappoint him, it would cause his downfall and ultimately bring about his death. In the rough and tumble fight with Detective Cudihee in October, 1894, Blanck repeatedly tried to cock and fire his .45 into the detective's midsection, but the wily lawman had his hand over the hammer, thus preventing the killer from cocking the revolver. As a result, Blanck was captured. In this instance, had Blanck been using a double-action revolver it would have been another story. The killer could have easily killed the detective, and likely Corbett as well, and escaped to do who knows what with two more notches on his gun.

Blanck's final affair was like a blind date, you have no choice in the matter. Following his escape from jail in March, 1895, Blanck was obliged to use the revolver he took from Jailer Yerbury. The only description was that it was a .38-calibre Colt. This indicates the revolver was likely a Colt Model 1877 "Lightning" Double Action revolver, the first double-action revolver made by Colt. It became a popular model and 168,849 were produced from 1877 until 1909.

161

Colt Model 1877 "Lightning" Double Action Revolver, .38 caliber.

Quoting from author Joseph Rosa, "for the most part their use was confined to the American police or similar organizations."[5]

In Tom Blanck's last confrontation, he seemed to regain his senses during the exchange of gunfire and put his first bullet into his target. The next three shots were extremely near misses, which again brings into play the harder trigger pull of a double-action revolver. The revolver was a six-shooter, but evidently Yerbury had the hammer sitting on a dead chamber, so Blanck's fifth shot, which likely was another narrow miss, was his last. In the end, Blanck's last object of love also let him down, it was empty and the killer died as a result. No doubt Tom Blanck would have been better off if he had given his love to a woman instead of a revolver.

[1] *Weiser Leader*, May 9, 1890.

[2] Charles Edward Chapel, *Gun Collector's Handbook Of Values*, Second Revised Edition, pp.208-09; Norm Flayderman, *Flayderman's Guide To Antique American Firearms*, 5th Edition, p.204.

[3] Donald B. Webster, Jr., *Suicide Specials*, pp.1-9; Flayderman, pp.368-70.

[4] Joseph G. Rosa, *Guns Of The American West*, pp. 121-124; Chapel, pp.143-44; Flayderman, pp.90-92.

[5] Chapel, p.149; Flayderman, pp.97-98; Rosa, p.134

Appendix

A Psychological Assessment of Tom Blanck

by David Hawley, M.A.

"She would get an ax and come up here and kill me."

The above words spoken by Tom Blanck regarding his mother is the key to what made him tick. This is the guide that enables one to peek into the mind of a cold-blooded, psychopathic killer.

Had Michael Hogan, Jr. aka Thomas Hamilton Blanck lived in the twentieth century, this concise summary and prognosis would have undoubtedly been presented by a forensic psychologist.

Summary and Recommendations: Tom Blanck, a twenty-four-year-old white, single male, has been convicted of murder in the first degree and has received the Death Sentence. He is currently housed in maximum custody on Death Row awaiting execution on December 7; however, an appeal has been filed by his attorneys. Based upon the results of this evaluation, Tom Blanck is an antisocial individual who is impulsive, unpredictable and will likely engage in assaultive, violent behavior in the future. It is unlikely that this individual would be responsive to treatment, thus his prognosis for change is extremely poor.

This conclusion reflects the dangerous pathology of Blanck's personality. There is nothing honorable about Tom Blanck. He would be seen today as an extremely dangerous, incorrigible, psychopathic criminal.

The remainder of this section will inform the reader how a psychologist determines an individual's character. In determining an assessment, many instruments are used; however, the most productive are psychological testing, past behavioral history and clinical interviews. In evaluating Tom Blanck, his answers to the myriad of newspaper reporter's questions can be substituted for clinical interviews since his past behavioral history is well documented. Although this review does not satisfy scientific method, an analysis regarding the development of Blanck's personality and character can be formulated.

Today, a psychopath or sociopath is classified as an Antisocial Personality Disorder. The tool psychologists use to classify a psychopath is the DSMIII (*Diagnostic and Statistical Manual of Mental Disorders, Third Edition, Revised*). The following are the ten personality characteristics and behavior patterns of a psychopath defined by the DSMIII:

(1) unable to consistently work, repeatedly absent, or abandoning jobs without plans for others; (2) failure to conform to social norms with respect to lawful behavior, i.e., committing criminal offenses; (3) irritable and aggressive, with history of repeated physical fights or assaults; (4) repeatedly fails to honor financial obligations; (5) fails to plan ahead, and is impulsive; (6) repeated lying, use of aliases, or "conning" others for personal profit or pleasure; (7) reckless regarding own or other's personal safety; (8) lacks ability to function as a responsible parent; (9) never sustains a monogamous relationship; (10) lacks remorse, and feels justified in having hurt, mistreated, or stolen from others.[1]

Tom Blanck moved from job to job, especially from 1890–1894, when he worked for four different railroad companies. Employed or not, he continued to commit criminal acts during the entire period.

A total of twenty antisocial acts were committed by Tom Blanck from 1890 until his death in 1895. During this period he was arrested on four different occasions, escaped three times and was released once. The most common of these offenses were murder, assault with a deadly weapon with intent to kill or inflicting serious bodily injury, and armed robbery.

Tom Blanck demonstrated his "short fuse" on numerous occasions. As "Slim Jim," Blanck shot at Judge Hanthorn for poking fun at him in 1890. In Amsterdam, New York, he was known as "Crazy Mike" because "no one wanted to engage with him in a rough and tumble fight, for he had done up six or seven people." Conductor Regan, from first-hand experience, stated he was a great fighter, "licking three men alone." In Montana, he shot a conductor in the thigh when he refused to give him his money, and in Seattle he threatened to throw his landlady over the banister when she asked for her house key.

All of Tom Blanck's travels were without purpose, he repeatedly lied and used at least eight aliases or nicknames. He conned others for personal profit or pleasure and mastered these qualities in his personality, using them to charm George Howe, G. W. Regan, the reporter for the *Post-Intelligencer*, and undoubtedly his jailhouse visitor, Mrs. Smith. All the men reflected upon Blanck's "good side," describing him as friendly, kind, generous, etc.

His recklessness and disregard for his or anyone else's safety is evident and is recorded throughout this book. Also, Blanck never had a monogamous relationship, and if he felt a need for sex he no doubt consorted with prostitutes. Blanck simply hated women, which is confirmed by his actions and his statements to George Howe.

Remorse? Consider these statements by Blanck: "Did I kill that fellow?", Blanck asked Frank McMurray. The boy answered, "Yes, you put it through his heart." "That's what I shot for," was Blanck's reply. The following was Blanck's reason for killing Birdwell, "Why didn't he give up the dough?" After getting the stuffing beat out of him by policeman Corbett, Blanck let the lawman have it. "I would kill you for fifty cents. If I meet you in hell I will run a pitchfork through you." Yet, to the reporter who asked, "Have you ever done much shooting?", Blanck said "No, not very much," and grinned.

One instance of Tom Blanck dodging financial obligations is when he left Tacoma owing his landlady rent money. Since Blanck was never a parent, responsible or otherwise, this is not relevant. On this scale from one to ten, Tom Blanck was a definite nine.

In Blanck's day, social histories interpreting child development, which is the key to his actions, were nonexistent, so there are no records that characterize his childhood. However, the following scenario is based upon the common factors found in the development of antisocial, sociopathic and psychopathic personalities. One more point, according to statistical data, between 10 and 20 percent of all convicted criminals and less than 20 percent of those imprisoned are diagnosed as antisocial personalities, or psychopaths/sociopaths.[2]

Tom Blanck was a survivor, from the first day of his life until the last, and it left him without human decency. Blanck's philosophy about life is embodied in his words that "death is nothing more than sleep." Yet, he undoubtedly learned and took to heart the idea that only the strong survive. He also believed in the axiom of do unto others before they do it unto you. Therefore, he simply uses things until there is no more need and then discards them.

As the eighth child in a family of ten children, he began his struggle for life. His mother was likely aggressive, domineering, inconsistent and punitive. Blanck's earliest memories of his mother must have centered on punishment for crying because he was hungry, dirty or frightened. Blanck's father was conceivably disinterested in him and would have been remembered solely for his harsh punishment of his children, especially if vexed or having bouts with the bottle. His brothers probably escaped into their worlds and offered little support to their brother because of their own needs. Through impatience and apathy, Blanck's mother likely delegated much of his care to his sisters. This would cause resentment, leading them to do no more than copy their mother's actions. To the outside world, the Hogan clan would have presented itself as a good Irish Catholic family, while the dark side remained secret. Tom Blanck's family was undoubtedly dysfunctional.

As Tom Blanck grew, so would his hatred for his mother and sisters. His feelings of affection, belonging and love were probably never accepted, so he replaced them with anger, hostility, restlessness and mischievousness.

Educationally, Blanck was undoubtedly an underachiever and disruptive in school. Rejection and punishment by his teachers would follow, which would increase his animosity toward women and those of authority. Becoming aware that aggressive behavior can bring rewards such as fear in others, power to control and the ability to take what you want, he likely began to exercise them against his schoolmates. He would also quickly learn to make sure he was bigger, stronger, quicker and smarter than those he intimidated. By the time he finished his common school education he would have been considered incorrigible.

Considering his actions as an adult, Blanck's development into adolescence would demonstrate that he had learned the fundamentals of a psychopathic lifestyle. Trust no one; avoid emotions at all costs; if it feels pleasurable then do it; carry the biggest stick. By the time Blanck reached the age of thirteen, his father undoubtedly rejected him and his mother would follow, openly expressing her dislike in words and deeds.

Thus, he was ready to find new territory to conquer–the railroad. Thomas Blanck knew about the men of the railroad and their riotous reputation. No doubt it was through the help of his older brother that he joined their rough and tumble fraternity. Through this association, Blanck would have enhanced his skills of manipulation and lying, and mastered physical violence through his fists. It would be during this period that he developed the ability to obliterate any recognition of emotional or physical pain, guilt, regret or fear. He became a self-sufficient, self-perpetuating, aggressively dangerous man. Tom Blanck graduated from a different kind of school.

When Blanck left home at age nineteen, he was either thrown out or voluntarily walked out on the Hogan family, and apparently never looked back. Eager to try his new skills, the soon-to-be killer headed west. He had learned his lessons well and practiced until he mastered them all.

Intellectually, Tom Blanck was gifted beyond the average man of his day, and his actions were always preceded by a decision. He robbed, stole, assaulted, lied, cheated, murdered and tortured because he wanted to, it excited him, yet it was not lasting. To Blanck, these acts were not morally wrong; if anything, he considered them normal, and they became ingrained in his mind as such. His callous remark that a man might as well be dead as alive is evidence that life meant nothing to him, and for this reason he did not fear death. This statement could be taken for a death wish, and, if so, he got his wish in the prime of life.

1 *Diagnostic and Statistical Manual of Mental Disorders, Third Edition, Revised*, pp.343-46.

2 John Altrocchi, *Abnormal Behavior*, p. 609; Benjamin Kleinmuntz, *Essentials Of Abnormal Psychology*, pp.292, 301; Benjamin B. Lahey and Anthony R. Ciminero, *Maladaptive Behavior: An Introduction to Abnormal Psychology*, pp.348, 353, 354.

Bibliography

Books:

Altrocchi, John, *Abnormal Behavior*, New York: Harcourt Brace Jovanovich, Inc., 1980.

Atlas of the City of Schenectady, New York, Philadelphia, Pa: D. L. Miller & A. H. Mueller, 1905.

Bagley, Clarence B., *History Of Seattle From The Earliest Settlements To The Present Time*, Volume II, Chicago: The S. J. Clarke Publishing Company, 1916.

Beginnings, Progress and Achievement in the Medical Work of King County, Washington, Seattle, 1930.

Butterfield, Roger, *The American Past*, New York: Simon and Schuster, 1947.

Chapel, Charles Edward, *Gun Collector's Handbook Of Values,* Second Revised Edition, New York: Coward-McCann Inc., 1951.

City Atlas of Schenectady, New York, Philadelphia: G. M. Hopkins, C.E., 1880.

Diagnostic and Statistical Manual of Mental Disorders, Third Edition, Revised, Washington, D.C.: American Psychiatric Association, 1987.

A Directory of Cemeteries and Funeral Homes in Washington State, Washington State Centennial Project of the Washington Interment Association and the Washington State Funeral Directors Association, 1989.

Dugan, Mark, *Tales Never Told Around The Campfire*, Athens, Ohio: Ohio University Press/Swallow Press, 1992.

Dugan, Mark, *The Making Of Legends*, Athens, Ohio: Ohio University Press/Swallow Press, 1997.

Dugan, Mark, and John Boessenecker, *The Grey Fox, The True Story Of Bill Miner, Last Of The Old-Time Bandits*, Norman: University of Oklahoma Press, 1992.

Duke, Thomas S., *Celebrated Criminal Cases Of America*, San Francisco, Cal.: James H. Barry Company, 1910.

Dullenty, Jim, *Harry Tracy: The Last Desperado*, Dubuque, Iowa: Kendall/Hunt Publishing Co., 1989.

Ficken, Robert E., *Washington: A Centennial History*, Seattle: University of Washington Press, 1988.

Flayderman, Norm, *Flayderman's Guide To Antique American Firearms*, 5th Edition, Northbrook, Illinois: DBI Books, 1990.

French, J. H., *Historical and Statistical Gazetteer of New York State*, Syracuse, N.Y.: R. P. Smith, 1860.

Kleinmuntz, Benjamin, *Essentials Of Abnormal Psychology*, New York: Harper and Row, 1974.

Lahey, Benjamin B., and Anthony R. Ciminero, *Maladaptive Behavior: An Introduction to Abnormal Psychology*, Glenview, Illinois: Scott, Foresman and Company, 1980.

Rosa, Joseph G., *Guns Of The American West*, New York: Crown Publishers, Inc., 1985.

Tindall, George Brown, *America, A Narrative History*, New York, London: W. W. Norton & Company, 1988.

Webster, Jr., Donald B., *Suicide Specials*, Stackpole Company, Harrisburg, Pennsylvania, 1958.

Articles and Periodicals:

DeLorme, Roland L., "The United States Bureau of Customs and Smuggling on Puget Sound, 1851 to 1913," *Prologue, Journal Of The National Archives*, Summer 1973, Volume 5, Number 2.

Unidentified Seattle newspaper articles: C. B. Bagley Scrapbook, Vol. 4. University of Washington Libraries, Seattle.

Unpublished Materials:

Markov, Richard W., "A Decade of Enforcement, The Chinese Exclusion And Whatcom County, 1890 to 1900," August 20, 1972. Western Washington University, Bellingham, Washington.

The Church Of Saint John The Baptist, Schenectady, New York, One Hundred Fiftieth Anniversary, 1830-1980. Saint John the Baptist Catholic Church, Schenectady.

GE Realty Plot Historic District, Schenectady, N.Y.: Realty Plot Association, 1980.

Historical Schenectady County, Schenectady County Historical Society, no date. Schenectady Public Library, Schenectady, N.Y.

Important Dates in the History of Schenectady, no date,

Schenectady Public Library, Schenectady, N.Y.

Papp, John, *Schenectady Then and Now*, Schenectady, N.Y.: Privately published, 1966.

Schenectady...Facts and Stuff, Prepared by Larry Hart, Schenectady County-City Historian, 1990. Schenectady Public Library, Schenectady, N.Y.

Public Documents:

1870 City of Schenectady, New York census.

1880 City of Schenectady, New York census.

1900 City of Schenectady, New York census.

Naturalization Petition No. 748, Michael Hogan. Schenectady County Clerk's Office, Schenectady, New York.

Schenectady City Directories, 1857-1880, 1887, 1890-91, 1895, 1901, 1906. Schenectady County Public Library, Schenectady, New York.

Criminal Case No. 1069, State of Washington vs. Thomas Blanck, Murder in the First Degree. Division of Archives and Records Management, Olympia, Washington.

Journal Of Proceedings Of County Commissioners, King County, Washington, Volume 9. King County Archives, Records and Election Division, Seattle, Washington.

King County Coroner's Reports, Vol. 2. King County Archives, Seattle, Washington.

King County Death Register, Record No. 1484, Blanck, Thos., March 21, 1895. Division of Archives and Records Management, Olympia, Washington.

King County Death Record, No. 131, Thomas Blanck, March 21, 1895. Division of Archives and Records Management, Olympia, Washington.

Potter's Field Record Book, Cemetery Records, 1912. Seattle-King County Department of Health, Seattle.

King County, Seattle, Washington Poor Farm Cremations, copied by Ron Cross, 1984. History Department, Seattle Public Library, Seattle.

Information on the Sheriffs of King County. Department of Public Safety, King County Sheriff's Department, King County Courthouse, Seattle.

Comet Lodge Cemetery Legal History. Comet Lodge Cemetery htm.

Comet Lodge Cemetery Burial List, King County Property Services Division, Seattle.

James A. Hamilton, Associates, 1965. *A Development Program King County Hospital Seattle, Washington*. Call no. 362.11097 J231D. Seattle Public Library.

Sherwood, M.D., Kenneth W., *The Development of King County Hospital*, 1970. Call no. R362.1 Sh58D. Seattle Public Library.

Annual Report of the King County Hospital For Year Ending December 31, 1917 and *Annual Report of the King County Hospital For Year Ending December 31, 1918*, both listed under the *Biennial Report Of The King County Hospital, 1917-1918*. Call no. R362 K59A 1917. Seattle Public Library.

Private Documents:

Baptismal Record, Michael Hogan, Jr. Saint John the Baptist Catholic Church, Schenectady, New York.

E. R. Butterworth and Sons Funeral Records, 1895. Butterworth Manning Ashmore, Funeral Directors, Seattle.

Newspapers:

The Argus (Seattle, Washington). University of Washington Libraries, Seattle.

Avant Courier (Bozeman, Montana). Montana Historical Society Library, Helena.

Bellingham Bay Express. Washington State Library, Olympia.

Daily Inter Mountain (Butte, Montana). Montana Historical Society Library, Helena.

The Daily Union (Schenectady, New York). Schenectady County Public Library, Schenectady, New York.

Evening Star (Schenectady, New York). Schenectady County Public Library, Schenectady, New York.

Helena Daily Herald. Montana Historical Society Library, Helena.

Helena Independent. Montana Historical Society Library, Helena.

Helena Weekly Herald. Montana Historical Society Library, Helena.

Kalama Bulletin. Washington State Library, Olympia.

Marysville Gazette. Montana Historical Society Library, Helena.

The Mountaineer (Marysville, Montana). Montana Historical Society Library, Helena.

New York Times. Schenectady County Public Library, Schenectady, New York.

Seattle Post-Intelligencer. Washington State Library, Olympia.

Seattle Telegraph (The articles from this newspaper are part of Criminal Case No. 1069, State of Washington vs. Thomas Blanck, Murder in the First Degree). Division of Archives and Records Management, Olympia, Washington.

Vancouver Daily World. British Columbia Archives and Records Center, Victoria.

The Weekly Leader (Port Townsend, Washington). Washington State Library, Olympia.

The Weekly World (Fairhaven, Washington). Washington State Library, Olympia.

Weiser Leader. Weiser Public Library, Weiser, Idaho.

Correspondence:

History of Seattle Cemeteries, provided by Dave Daly, President of Evergreen-Washelli, (Cemeteries and Funeral Home), Seattle, Washington.

Letter to author, dated July 13, 1992, Richard Engeman, University of Washington Libraries, Seattle.

Interviews:

Derick, Jr., M.D., Dr. William A., Appalachian State University, Boone, North Carolina, May 23, 1992.

Newell, M.D., Dr. Josephine, Raleigh, North Carolina, June 22, 1992.

Nordstrom, M.D., Dr. Carl R., Appalachian State University, Boone, North Carolina, May 8, June 11, 1992.

Powell, Dr. Geraldine, Asheville, North Carolina, July 7, 1992.
Townsend, Mr. Jerry, Bass & Smith Funeral Home, Hickory, North Carolina, October 10, 2002.

Index